How Well Does Your Child Do Math?

A Step-by-Step Assessment of Your Child's Math Skills and Techniques to Develop Them

By
Ann Cook

Illustrated by Holly Forsyth

CAREER PRESS
3 Tice Road
P.O. Box 687
Franklin Lakes, NJ 07417
1-800-CAREER-1
201-848-0310 (NJ and outside U.S.)
FAX: 201-848-1727

HOW WELL DOES YOUR CHILD DO MATH?
ISBN 1-56414-302-3, $9.99
Cover design by Robert Howard
Illustrated by Holly Forsyth
Printed in the U.S.A. by Book-mart Press

To order this title by mail, please include price as noted above, $2.50 handling per order, and $1.50 for each book ordered. Send to: Career Press, Inc., 3 Tice Road, P.O. Box 687, Franklin Lakes, NJ 07417.

Or call toll-free 1-800-CAREER-1 (in NJ and Canada: 201-848-0310) to order using VISA or MasterCard, or for further information on books from Career Press.

Library of Congress Cataloging-in-Publication Data

Cook, Ann, 1954-
    How well does your child do math? : a step-by-step assessment of your child's math skills / by Ann Cook.
        p.   cm.
    Includes index.
    ISBN 1-56414-302-3   (pbk.)
    1. Mathematics--Examinations, questions, etc. 2. Mathematical ability--Evaluation.   I. Title.
QA43.C775   1997
372.7'2--dc21   97-13344
                                                              CIP

For Nate

Special thanks to Susan Greenberg.

For referral to a qualified testing or tutoring center, call 800-457-4255 or e-mail testing kids@earthlink.net

Contents

Introduction

You've probably noticed that times have changed since you were in school. The math work your son or daughter brings home seems quite different from what *you* were learning at that age. Children today are expected to be more familiar with the underlying concepts than with the rote memorization of math facts. You're left to wonder: "What is normal for a child in my daughter's grade?" or "What are the national standards in arithmetic?"

You also begin to worry that report cards and scores on standardized tests aren't telling you enough about how your son or daughter is *really* performing academically. After all, news reports are assaulting you with discouraging statistics about American education. In 1996, the National Assessment of Educational Progress (NAEP), an arm of the U.S. Department of Education that monitors academic achievement through periodic testing of 4th, 8th, and 12th graders, found that, of the nation's 4th graders, 36 percent were not mastering basic math skills, such as measuring something longer than a ruler, and 38 percent cannot solve a problem involving money or identify the fraction that represents the shaded portion of a rectangle. By the 4th grade, 100 percent of students should be testing at or above basic-skill level, but the latest NAEP math test results showed that the state with the highest percentage (Maine) had only 75 percent of 4th grade students at or above that level. The 1996 assessment also showed that almost 40 percent of 8th graders still lack even basic number skills.

It's no longer safe to assume that everything must be okay if your child continues to be promoted, as there is often an unpublicized "no-fail" policy in schools, where children are routinely advanced to the next grade when they have not achieved even a remedial level in the previous grade. The thinking was that "flunking" stigmatized a child and separated him from his peer group, and that the child would continue to do poorly and possibly end up not graduating. It was deemed preferable to put a child into the next grade and give additional academic support. Unfortunately, this support was not always available, but the policy was in place and the child would be passed along nonetheless. So how do you make sure that your child is on the right track—that he doesn't become a part of these bleak statistics?

You *can* identify specific learning problems by checking the results of whatever standardized test your child is required to take in school every year. But these tests vary from state to state, and not all teachers support the findings. Part of the problem is that America, unlike most advanced nations, does not have a national curriculum. The states' constitutional right to establish their own educational systems means that some schools have a wonderful school curriculum, but others leave much to be desired. It also means that students' annual standardized test scores might only reflect their performance on a regional level.

Furthermore, school report cards indicate only your child's *overall* performance. If you see a low grade in math on your 4th grader's report card, you know only that there's a problem—not what the problem is. You can, of course, schedule a conference with the teacher, but if the teacher is simply not strong in math, it will be difficult to isolate the problem.

But what, if you could figure out that your 4th grader can add, subtract, multiply, and divide with 80 percent accuracy, but is struggling with fractions? This is what *How Well Does Your Child Do Math?* can help you do. Then, you can work with your child with workbooks, discussions, games, and exercises.

Why I wrote this book

As a parent, I had the same concerns you do. When my son was in the 2nd grade, I noticed that he and his classmates were picking up the concepts of arithmetic with the classroom manipulative exercises, but there was little or no emphasis on memorizing sums and differences.

Current educational theory has often caused math books to be eliminated from the curriculum, replacing them with manipulative blocks and beads. The consequence of this is that many children, in spite of being able to explain the underlying concepts, can't do addition and subtraction quickly and accurately. This carried over into 3rd grade, where the children understood that if seven children each have eight toys, they could line up seven rows of eight blocks and count them up to find the sum or to determine that it was a multiplication problem. However, to answer the question, "What is seven times eight?" it is common practice for American 3rd graders to be encouraged to use a times table chart to look up the answer. This handicaps children because they will be forced to rely on these charts permanently, whereas when they memorize the information, they own it for life.

Because of my concerns about my son's performance in math, I had my son tested at a local math tutoring center and found that his arithmetic skills were at least a year below grade level. Because this particular center focuses on mastery of each level, there is a great deal of repetition. In the current vernacular of "guess and check" math proponents, this is called "drill and kill."

At that point, I had already put together *How Well Does Your Child Read?*, so I realized that something like it could also be used to monitor a child's math skills on an ongoing basis. As a linguist and the director of American Accent Training, a nationwide program to teach foreign-born students to speak standard American English, I had experience creating diagnostic analyses and other kinds of tests. I used what I knew about testing to create a math "inventory" to test my own son, as well as with the children in the ACE (After Class Enrichment) Program I had founded at the local elementary school.

This became the foundation for *How Well Does Your Child Do Math?*, which led me to write another book featuring tests to help you assess your child's writing performance, *How Well Does Your Child Write?*

The material for my diagnostic tests has been garnered from a number of reliable sources. I studied the NAEP's assessments of American students' abilities in reading, mathematics, and writing. It has been conducting such tests since 1969, ranking the results of the tests by state and providing appropriate achievement goals for each age and grade. I also relied on the Third International Math and Science Study (TIMSS), which is an assessment of the math and science achievement of students in the United States and 40 other nations; books on test research; advice from the director of a Kumon Math Center; and online information. (See page 179 for online resources.)

Finally, my diagnostic tests went through a series of trial runs with children, in addition to being evaluated by experienced elementary school teachers and reviewed by an educational therapist.

How to use this book

How Well Does Your Child Do Math? contains a mathematics diagnostic/placement test for children in kindergarten through grade 5. It will help you determine the grade level at which your child has mastered the concepts and computation of elementary arithmetic. You can use this assessment to target areas that may need additional work. Or, if you discover that your child is performing at or above his grade level, this book can allay your doubts about your child's ability and help you guide him to the next level.

The book contains the following sections:

♦ Definitions of the terms used in kindergarten through 5th grade math, such as *lowest common denominator, integer,* and *fraction* (pages 25-27).

♦ A learning style pre-test to determine whether your child's learning style is primarily auditory (does your child acquire and retain information by what he hears?) or visual (does your child acquire and retain information by what he sees)? (pages 19-20).

♦ Test-taking tips and tricks (pages 21-24).

♦ A shapes, numbers, and counting assessment for kindergartners, testing the ability to recognize and write numbers (pages 30-33).

♦ Arithmetic assessments for children in grades 1 through 5, testing knowledge of numbers, time and money, patterning, addition, subtraction, fractions, word problems, charting, division, estimation, and averaging (pages 34-64).

♦ A chart to help you track your child's progress (pages 65-66).

♦ A chapter on grade level guidelines to familiarize you with math skills that are or should be covered at each grade level, along with difficulties your child may have and ways to overcome them (pages 67-134).

♦ Reassessments (pages 135-170).

♦ An answer key for some of the more advanced test questions (pages 70-71).

♦ An explanation of the NAEP's latest math assessment, with a chart showing children's performance in individual states (pages 173-177).

♦ Listings of educational services and online resources (pages 179-188).

The mathematics assessment

For many years, educators had students memorize sums, equations, and times tables without relating their understanding of math facts to practical application, such as figuring out a baseball player's batting average or the tax on a long list of grocery items.

More recently, teachers were trained to teach concepts to children that would do away with laborious rote memorization. The TIMSS, however, found that American children may be *introduced* to more concepts than students in much higher-scoring nations, but they do not *master* these concepts. The highest students in America ranked lower than the lowest students in Asia, according to the study.

Studies show that American students are weak in computation, concepts, and application. Educators have been divided on the best way to teach students these skills—"guess and check" or "drill and kill." Guess and check, another term for estimation, gives students the skills necessary to make a ballpark judgment about "how much" or "how many" of something. The proponents of guess and check feel that if children have an understanding of the principles, pure memorization of facts is not necessary, especially with the availability of calculators. Drill and kill is straight memorization of math facts. Its proponents say that arithmetic has no exceptions, so knowing the rules makes learning the concepts easier and faster because the child is focusing on ideas, with the underlying foundation having already been laid.

Educators are now coming to the conclusion that the guess and check/drill and kill debate is not an "either/or" situation. Memorizing the fundamental rules of addition, subtraction, multiplication, and division is the first logical step, followed by applying the basic concepts to higher math. This, then, is how the diagnostic test in this book is organized.

Scoring the assessment

In these tests, the goal is for your child to succeed at a minimum of 80 percent accuracy. As you give each test, check the bottom of the page for the allowable number of errors, which will depend on the number of items in the section.

Using the chart on page 65, put a check mark next to the category each time your child passes a particular level. If your child misses more than the allowable number, leave the chart blank and stop the testing at that point. Work with your child on that concept until he masters it. Then reassess him at a later date—two to three months (see page 135 for reassessments).

For example, check marks up to single digit addition indicate that your child has learned his numbers up to 100 and can add up to 9 + 9, but doesn't fully understand carrying in addition, or single digit subtraction. This is an indicator of his grade level and of the particular functions that he needs to practice.

Because it is frustrating to be tested on unknown or half-understood material, its is not recommended that you go beyond the specific point where your child is unable to succeed. But it must be noted that many children are able to succeed at levels higher than at which they are having difficulty. For example, some children are able to do single digit multiplication (a 3rd grade skill) while still struggling with borrowing in double digit subtraction (a 2nd grade skill). Therefore parents should use their own discretion in deciding how much further in the testing they wish to proceed, based on the abilities of their child.

Math skills consist of sequential building blocks. Arithmetic skills are taught in a particular order because more advanced skills require knowledge of the basic skills for mastery. Although a national arithmetic curriculum has not been established in America, and standards may vary from school to school, the assessments in this book will be a good general indicator of your child's math level.

Is this an intelligence test?

No. It is extremely important to remember that early or late arithmetic skills are not an indicator of intelligence. Through practice, any child can learn the four functions using the nine integers and zero. Late bloomers can be given the tools to develop quick and accurate skills. Children need to be helped through the transition from arithmetic and basic comprehension of it, to enjoying and relating to the numbers in their daily lives.

Before you begin

Before you plunge into the rest of this book, are you sure that no physical or learning impediments are hampering your child's ability to do math? For example, has your child's eyesight been checked recently? If he or she has been displaying learning problems, have you ruled out the possibility of Attention Deficit Disorder (ADD) or dyslexia? Only after you've determined that your child is ready, willing, and *able* to learn should you give the diagnostic test to determine what your child's math level is and what you may do to improve it.

How to give the test

Set aside 20 minutes alone with your child in a quiet room. Make sure there are no distractions—turn off the TV, and never try to give the test just before a big soccer match or gymnastics practice.

Tell your child that this will only take a few minutes and that the results will help make math more enjoyable. Stress that there's no pressure, no punishment, no failing.

Depending on the age of your child, the two of you can sit side by side while you score and he answers the questions. Direct your child's attention to the numbers on the page, not the marks you're making. Some children can become anxious if they pay too much attention to your scoring.

Students in kindergarten through 2nd grade should be monitored closely because they cannot always read the instructions, and they will have a greater tendency to get sidetracked. Independent study starts in the 3rd grade, so children at the 3rd grade level or higher can have greater autonomy during the test. (Of course, the behavior of individual children can vary greatly, so there will be exceptions to this.)

For younger children (kindergartners to 2nd graders), the test will take from one minute, because they don't know numbers well, to 20 minutes. I recommend a 20-minute limit to combat the "fatigue factor"; boredom or exasperation can lower children's scores even in subjects they know better than the characters on the latest Saturday morning TV cartoons. Older children (grades 3 to 5) can take the test within 20 minutes to an hour, depending on their motivation, cooperation, and stamina.

What if your child takes longer? Well, computational skills need to be quick and accurate. If your child takes too much time, he doesn't know the material. At that point, the test should be stopped and the previous lessons drilled. If your child is spending a lot of time on one math problem, remember a good rule of math test-taking: Never let the clock run out on 20 questions because you're stuck on one. If your child is spending an inordinate amount of time on one problem, this could mean the child hasn't grasped that "type" of problem just yet. Encourage him to move on to other problems and come back to that one later.

What to do after the test

Once your child reaches the point in the test where the questions are beyond his grade level, you can end the test. The answer key is at the back of the book. Turn to the scoring section and determine the grade level that corresponds to your child's score. Once that has been determined, consult the chapter on standards for each grade level—kindergarten through 5th. Here you will find suggestions on helping your child with any areas of difficulty that have been identified in the assessment. These standards and guidelines can help you with remediation if your child scores below grade level. This chapter also introduces you to the next level or levels if your child is at or above grade level.

One of the primary functions of the test is to familiarize you with the materials that should be taught at each level. Once that familiarization has taken place, you can seek out appropriate materials for your child.

You can obtain flash cards or worksheets that are appropriate to your child's level by calling Matrix at 800-457-4255. Keep in mind that when practicing by themselves, children need materials that are interesting and challenging, not overwhelming. Also, it's okay if your child wants to do the same easy problems over and over. That's an excellent way to reinforce the basics and build math confidence and fluency.

Retesting

If you feel your child has made progress after the work you've done together, you can test him again. Or even if he performed at the appropriate level the first time around, you still may want to give the test periodically to monitor his skills. In the first case, your child needs to be tested on the same material as before, but he may have memorized the answers. So you should use the reevaluations in the back of the book. In the second scenario, you can just pick up at the point in the test where your child left off.

Each time you give the test, record the date so you can chart your child's progress. Continue giving the test until your child is at or above grade level.

How often should you retest your child? This depends upon the age of the child. A 5-year-old who is just learning his numbers could be tested every four to six months, while a 7-year-old, who needs to master the concepts for school, could be tested every two to four months. Children who are on track could be tested at the beginning and end of each school year.

Now, if you're ready (and your child is ready), let's find out how well your child can do math!

Learning Style
Pre-test

It is helpful for parents to understand their child's learning style. Some children's learning strength is *auditory*—they acquire and retain information by what they hear; others learn *visually*—by what they see; and some children learn the best in a *tactile* or *kinesthetic* way—by physically touching or manipulating the objects that they are counting.

This quick test will help determine if your child's learning style is markedly auditory or visual.

Auditory Sequential Memory

Say the groups of digits at a rate of one digit every two seconds. Then ask your child to repeat the digits back. Keep adding a new set until she makes a mistake.

1. 5-2-1
2. 6-3-5-8
3. 2-5-4-8-7
4. 4-9-1-6-2-8
5. 3-8-9-1-6-2-4

Visual Sequential Memory

Show the digits to your child, allowing two seconds for each digit. Then remove or cover the paper and ask her to repeat the digits back. Keep adding a new set until she makes a mistake.

1. 6-8-2
2. 4-1-5-9
3. 6-5-1-8-4
4. 8-1-3-6-7-0
5. 7-8-2-1-0-6-9

Interpretation

Most people use a combination of learning styles, but usually one is dominant. If your child shows a marked preference for *visual memory,* she would benefit by practicing math with flash cards, pictures and graphs.

If your child shows a marked preference for *auditory memory,* she would benefit by practicing math out loud—chanting the times tables, reciting the problem and answer, or listening to a tape.

A child with a marked preference for *kinesthetic memory* would benefit by practicing math with manipulatives—blocks, pieces of paper, coins, and beads.

The main point is that not all approaches work for all people. Experiment with different approaches and see what works best for your child.

Test-taking
Techniques

There are two elements to taking a test successfully. Most important, of course, is knowing the information. The other is knowing the test.

Tests are written according to basic standards and practices. This is why school tests are called *standardized*. It is very helpful for your child to be familiar with test standards and formats before starting a test, so that he can focus on the content, rather than on the test itself. Here are some basic guidelines:

First, look the whole test over. This includes noting how much time you have for the test, how long the test is, and what kind of test it is—multiple choice or fill-in-the-blank. In the 4th and 5th grades, word problems get longer and more difficult, and often you have to "show your work." Many a 10-year-old has gotten to the end of a math test with 10 minutes left to go, only to be dismayed to find two pages of complicated word problems!

Next, put your pencil down and read the instructions. Then read them again.

Following this, prioritize to determine if questions are equally weighted. If some questions are worth only 1 point and others are worth 10 points, spend more time and energy on the more heavily weighted problems.

Next, know *what you need to solve for* in the problem. If it is a word problem, write a number equation to help you solve it. Circle each number in the word problem and underline what function should be used. Make sure that the number equation matches exactly and every element is accounted for. An example would be:

Bobby had <u>three</u> apples; he ate [minus] <u>one</u> and gave [minus] <u>two</u> to Cindy. How many were left?

3 – 1 = 2 and 2 – 2 = 0

One of the easiest techniques for a multiple choice test is the process of elimination. If there are four possibilities, chances are that one of them will be way off base, so first, eliminate the ridiculous. Another one will probably be fairly unlikely. Cross that one out, too. Of the two remaining, both will be possibilities, but since you've eliminated the clearly wrong answers, you can concentrate on finding the correct one of two, instead of the correct one of four. For example, these are questions from a typical 3rd grade standardized math test:

The chart below shows the results of a survey when 20 students were asked to choose their favorite ice cream. Which flavor was the favorite?

vanilla	cherry	peach	mint

❑ cherry   ❑ peach
❑ mint   ❑ vanilla

This is reading and interpreting a graph, which is well within the 3rd grade skill range. The first step is to *eliminate the ridiculous*. Because the question asks for the favorite ice cream, you can immediately eliminate the visibly smaller segments of *peach* and *vanilla*. This leaves you with two fairly similar segments for *mint* and *cherry*. This is where you look for additional information. Because *cherry* has 8 grids shaded and *mint* has only 7, then this would indicate that *cherry* was the favorite flavor.

Another excellent technique is to convert numbers into pictures. This will help you visualize the problem.

Mark buys 24 bags of potato chips. The chips come 8 bags to a box. How many boxes of chips does Mark buy?

   ❑ 32   ❑ 3

   ❑ 192   ❑ 4

You know that Mark bought 24 bags. You also know that there are groups of 8 (8 bags to a box). Make 32 little marks for the total number of *bags* and group them by 8 for the number of *boxes*:

You can see that there are 3 groups. Whenever the process involves counting smaller groups within a whole, it will probably be a division problem: **24 ÷ 8 = 3.**

You can also eliminate the ridiculous. You can immediately eliminate 192 and 32, because if the bags are *within* the boxes, you will obviously end up with fewer boxes than there are bags. The two reasonable answers are 3 and 4, which are easily checked by doing division, and double checked by doing the reverse operation, multiplication (**3 x 8 = 24**).

Once you have figured out how to do a certain problem, look for more problems of that type and use the same technique to solve it.

Test-taking tips

1. Look the whole test over.
2. Prioritize.
3. Read the instructions.
4. Read the instructions again.
5. Make sure that you have scratch paper for working out problems.
6. After you read each problem, look for key words that tell you what kind of computation is needed, such as *more than, less than, greatest, least, closes, between,* etc.
7. Make sure that you know *what you need to solve for* in the problem, for example, how much is left, how much the total is, and so on.
8. In multiple choice questions, eliminate the obviously wrong answers and then be sure to check all possible correct answers. Don't choose the first one that looks likely.

Terms You Should Know

Four functions

Addition The process of uniting two or more numbers into one sum, represented by the symbol **+**.

Subtraction To take away (withdraw) one number or quantity from another, represented by the symbol **−**.

Multiplication Adding a number (the *multiplicand*) to itself a certain number of times in order to find the *product*, represented by the symbol **x**.

Division How many times one quantity is contained in another—the inverse of multiplication, represented by the symbol **÷**.

Fractions

Numerator The top number in a fraction.

Denominator The bottom number in a fraction.

LCD *Lowest Common Denominator* The least common multiple of the denominators of a set of fractions.

Common Fraction A fraction having an integer as a numerator and an integer as a denominator. Also called a vulgar fraction.

Proper Fraction A numerical fraction in which the numerator is less than the denominator (2/3).

Improper Fraction A fraction in which the numerator is larger than or equal to the denominator (3/2).

Mixed Number A whole number and a fraction (1 ½).

Decimal Fraction A linear array of integers that represents a fraction, every decimal place indicating a multiple of a negative power of 10. For example, the decimal $0.1 = 1/10$; $0.12 = 12/100$; $0.003 = 3/1000$.

Decimal Point A dot written in a decimal number to indicate where the place values change from whole numbers to tenths, hundredths, thousandths, etc. of a number.

Reciprocal A number related to another in such a way that when multiplied together their product is 1. For example, the reciprocal of 2/3 is 3/2.

Numbers

Digit One of the ten Arabic number symbols, 0 through 9.

Number Any quantity, including positive numbers (1), negative numbers (-1), zero (0), fractions (½), percentages (10%), and decimals (.5). A number is made up of digits.

Whole Number Any of the set of numbers including zero and all negative and positive multiples of 1.

Integer Any positive whole numbers (1, 2, 3...), negative whole numbers (-1, -2, -3...), and zero (0). This excludes fractions, percentages and decimals.

Natural Number Any positive whole number, excluding zero.

Factor One of two or more quantities that divides a given quantity without a remainder. For example, number 2 has two factors, 2 and 1, because $2 \div 1 = 2$ and $2 \div 2 = 1$. Number 6 has four factors, 1 and 6, 2 and 3.

Prime Number A number having only two factors—itself and 1. Example: the number 7, which can only be divided by itself and one to end up with no remainder.

Composite Number A number having more than two factors.

Geometry

Point A dimensionless geometric object having no properties except location.

Line The shortest distance between two points.

Ray A straight line extending from a point. Also called half-line.

Right Angle An angle formed by the perpendicular intersection of two straight lines. An angle of 90°.

Acute angle An angle less than 90°.

Obtuse Angle An angle greater than 90° and less than 180°.

Vertex The point at which the sides of an angle intersect.

Diameter A straight line segment passing through the center of a figure, especially of a circle or sphere, and terminating at the periphery.

Circumference The boundary line of a circle.

Cube An object having six equal square faces.

Octagon A closed plane figure bounded by eight line segments and eight angles.

Polygon A closed plane figure bounded by three or more line segments.

Congruent Coinciding exactly when superimposed. The same size and shape.

Horizontal Parallel to the horizon

Vertical At right angles to the horizon; upright.

Parallel Two or more straight lines that do not intersect.

Perpendicular A line at right angles to a given line.

Assessments

Kindergarten
through
Fifth Grade

Shapes & Sizes   *Kindergarten*

1. Color the mailbox that is the biggest.

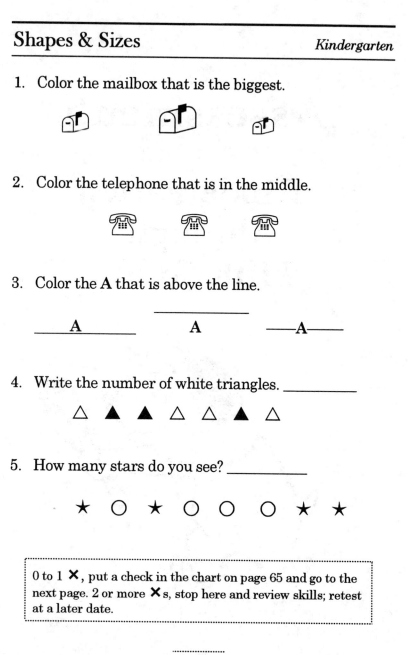

2. Color the telephone that is in the middle.

3. Color the A that is above the line.

4. Write the number of white triangles. _____

5. How many stars do you see? _____

---

0 to 1 ✗, put a check in the chart on page 65 and go to the next page. 2 or more ✗s, stop here and review skills; retest at a later date.

Patterns & Counting   *Kindergarten*

1. Draw a line from the number to the group that it matches.

2. How many balloons do you see? _____

3. Color the circle red, the square blue, and the triangle yellow.

4. Color the matching shape.

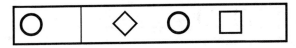

5. Circle the group that has the most in it.

0 to 1 ✗, put a check in the chart on page 65 and go to the next page. 2 or more ✗s, stop here and review skills; retest at a later date.

Recognizing Numbers 1-10 *Kindergarten*

Have your child say each number.

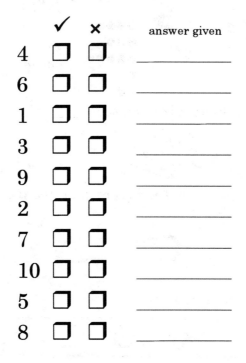

	✓	✗	answer given
4	☐	☐	_____
6	☐	☐	_____
1	☐	☐	_____
3	☐	☐	_____
9	☐	☐	_____
2	☐	☐	_____
7	☐	☐	_____
10	☐	☐	_____
5	☐	☐	_____
8	☐	☐	_____

✓ = immediate response   ✗ = slow or incorrect response
0 to 2 ✗ s, put a check in the chart on page 65 and go to the next page. 3 or more ✗ s, stop here and review skills; retest at a later date.

Writing Numbers 1-10   *Kindergarten*

Have your child write each number on his own, in order. Start with 0 and work up to 10.

_____

_____

_____

_____

_____

_____

_____

_____

_____

_____

0 to 2 ✖ s, put a check in the chart on page 65 and go to the next page. 3 or more ✖ s, stop here and review skills; retest at a later date.

Recognizing Numbers 1-100 *First Grade*

Have your child say each number.

	✓	✗	answer given
42	☐	☐	_____
61	☐	☐	_____
57	☐	☐	_____
38	☐	☐	_____
94	☐	☐	_____
12	☐	☐	_____
45	☐	☐	_____
24	☐	☐	_____
78	☐	☐	_____
83	☐	☐	_____

✓ = immediate response   ✗ = slow or incorrect response
0 to 2 ✗ s, put a check in the chart on page 65 and go to
the next page. 3 or more ✗ s, stop here and review skills;
retest at a later date.

Writing Numbers 1-100 *First Grade*

Dictate the following numbers to your child and have him write them on the line.

fifty five _____

twenty six _____

sixty seven _____

twenty one _____

thirty nine _____

forty eight _____

seventeen _____

seventy _____

one hundred and six _____

eighty three _____

0 to 2 ✗s, put a check in the chart on page 65 and go to the next page. 3 or more ✗s, stop here and review skills; retest at a later date.

Signs & Skip Counting

First Grade

Fill in the blanks by skip counting by 2s.

1. 5   7   _____   11   13

2. 12   _____   _____   _____   20

Fill in the blanks by counting by 3s.

3. 2   _____   8   _____   14   _____

4. 3   _____   _____   12   _____

Put the correct sign on the line (>, <, =).

5. 8 _____ 6

6. 0 _____ 3

7. 15 _____ 14

8. 4 _____ 2+2

9. 11 _____ 15

10. 36 _____ 36

0 to 2 ✘s, put a check in the chart on page 65 and go to the next page. 3 or more ✘s, stop here and review skills; retest at a later date.

Sequencing & Ordering   *First Grade*

Answer the following questions.

1. What is one more than 69? _____
2. What is one less than 30? _____
3. What is ten more than 23? _____
4. What is ten less than 58? _____
5. What is five more than 45? _____

Fill in the numbers that would come next.

6. 2 4 6 _____ _____
7. 25 35 45 _____ _____
8. 300 400 500 _____ _____
9. 296 297 298 _____ _____

Circle the larger number in each set.

10. 4   8   12. 21   12
11. 1   11   13. 11   2

Rewrite these numbers in order from the largest to the smallest.

14.   8   5   11   4   6

_____ _____ _____ _____ _____

15.   125   100   90   45   62

_____ _____ _____ _____ _____

0 to 3 ✗s, put a check in the chart on page 65 and go to the next page. 4 or more ✗s, stop here and review skills; retest at a later date.

Single & Double Digit Addition   *First Grade*

Solve the following problems.

1.   9
     + 1

6.   72
     + 19

2.   3
     + 6

7.   42
     + 37

3.   6
     + 2

8.   54
     + 35

4.   3
     + 4

9.   36
     + 43

5.   4
     + 4

10.   72
     + 17

---

0 to 2 ✖s, put a check in the chart on page 65 and go to the next page. 3 or more ✖s, stop here and review skills; retest at a later date.

Single & Double Digit Subtraction   *First Grade*

Solve the following problems.

1.   6
   − 3

6.   87
  − 11

2.   9
   − 5

7.   39
  − 28

3.   29
  − 14

8.   73
  − 51

4.   8
   − 3

9.   98
  − 55

5.   7
   − 4

10.   25
  − 12

0 to 2 ✗ s, put a check in the chart on page 65 and go to the next page. 3 or more ✗ s, stop here and review skills; retest at a later date.

Time & Money

First Grade

Answer the following questions.

1. What time is it? _____

2. Draw hands on the clock to show 7:00.

3. About how long would it take to eat dinner?

   ❑ 3 minutes   ❑ 30 minutes

4. About how long would it take to comb your hair?

   ❑ 1 minute   ❑ 1 hour

5. How many cents is each coin? Write the amount below the coin.

_____   _____   _____   _____

> 0 to 1 ✖, put a check in the chart on page 65 and go to the next page. 2 or more ✖s, stop here and review skills; retest at a later date.

Patterns

Copy the pattern.

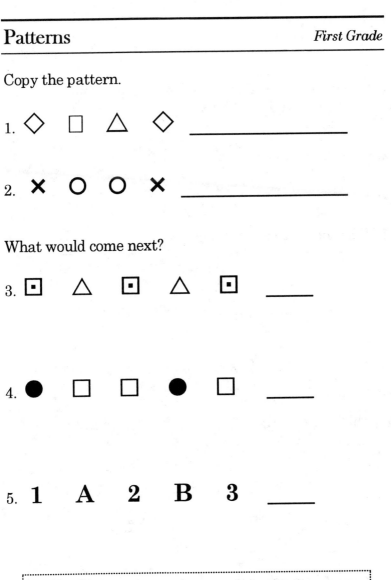

1. ◇　□　△　◇　_____

2. ✖　○　○　✖　_____

What would come next?

3. ▣　△　▣　△　▣　____

4. ●　□　□　●　□　____

5. **1**　**A**　**2**　**B**　**3**　____

0 to 1 ✖, put a check in the chart on page 65 and go to the next page. 2 or more ✖s, stop here and review skills; retest at a later date.

Time & Money

Second Grade

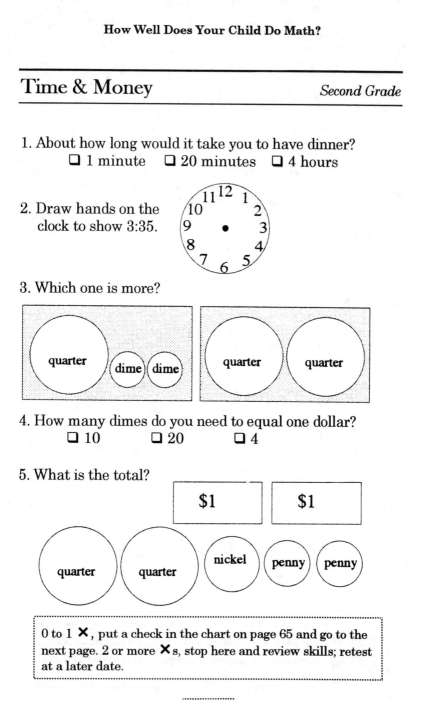

1. About how long would it take you to have dinner?
   ❑ 1 minute ❑ 20 minutes ❑ 4 hours

2. Draw hands on the clock to show 3:35.

3. Which one is more?

4. How many dimes do you need to equal one dollar?
   ❑ 10   ❑ 20   ❑ 4

5. What is the total?

   $1 $1

   quarter quarter nickel penny penny

0 to 1 ✖, put a check in the chart on page 65 and go to the next page. 2 or more ✖s, stop here and review skills; retest at a later date.

Computation with Regrouping   *Second Grade*

Solve the following problems.

1.   29
      + 32

6.   75
      − 56

2.   81
      + 25

7.   65
      − 48

3.   76
      + 28

8.   27
      − 19

4.   55
      + 37

9.   43
      − 38

5.   43
      + 27

10.   44
       − 16

0 to 2 ✖ s, put a check in the chart on page 65 and go to the next page. 3 or more ✖ s, stop here and review skills; retest at a later date.

Simple Fractions

Second Grade

Look at each picture and write the fraction, with the numerator represented by the white space. A sample is given.

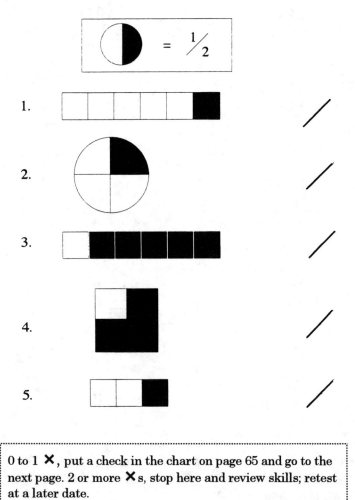

3 Digit Mixed Computation   *Second Grade*

Solve the following problems.

1. $\begin{array}{r} 446 \\ + 575 \\ \hline \end{array}$

6. $\begin{array}{r} 748 \\ - 669 \\ \hline \end{array}$

2. $\begin{array}{r} 723 \\ - 408 \\ \hline \end{array}$

7. $\begin{array}{r} 512 \\ + 389 \\ \hline \end{array}$

3. $\begin{array}{r} 687 \\ + 245 \\ \hline \end{array}$

8. $\begin{array}{r} 300 \\ - 129 \\ \hline \end{array}$

4. $\begin{array}{r} 425 \\ + 398 \\ \hline \end{array}$

9. $\begin{array}{r} 801 \\ - 799 \\ \hline \end{array}$

5. $\begin{array}{r} 916 \\ - 787 \\ \hline \end{array}$

10. $\begin{array}{r} 122 \\ + 188 \\ \hline \end{array}$

0 to 2 ✕ s, put a check in the chart on page 65 and go to the next page. 3 or more ✕ s, stop here and review skills; retest at a later date.

Word Problems

Second Grade

Read the following questions and mark the correct answer.

1. If a train travels 10 miles east and then 22 miles north, how many miles has it gone in all?

   _____

2. If a farmer has 17 eggs for sale, and someone buys 9, how many eggs are left?

   _____

3. 7 children go to a party and play in the back yard. 3 children go into the kitchen for some juice. 2 children go into the house to rest. How many children are left in the back yard?

   _____

4. Write the following words in number form: one hundred forty two _____

5. Write the following words in number form: four hundred eighty three _____

> 0 to 1 ✘, put a check in the chart on page 65 and go to the next page. 2 or more ✘ s, stop here and review skills; retest at a later date.

Single Digit Multiplication/Division *Third Grade*

Solve the following problems.

1. $\begin{array}{r} 7 \\ \times\,2 \\ \hline \end{array}$

6. $9 \times 5 =$

2. $2\overline{)8}$

7. $4 \div 2 =$

3. $\begin{array}{r} 7 \\ \times\,3 \\ \hline \end{array}$

8. $9 \times 7 =$

4. $3\overline{)6}$

9. $8 \div 2 =$

5. $\begin{array}{r} 3 \\ \times\,6 \\ \hline \end{array}$

10. $5 \times 0 =$

0 to 2 ✖ s, put a check in the chart on page 65 and go to the next page. 3 or more ✖ s, stop here and review skills; retest at a later date.

Double Digit Multiplication/Division *Third Grade*

Solve the following problems.

1. 12
    x 2

6. 3 ⟌ 27

2. 8 ⟌ 32

7. 9 ⟌ 45

3. 48
    x 3

8. 69
    x 4

4. 6 ⟌ 36

9. 8 ⟌ 56

5. 37
    x 6

10. 98
    x 6

0 to 2 ✗ s, put a check in the chart on page 65 and go to the next page. 3 or more ✗ s, stop here and review skills; retest at a later date.

Time & Money   *Third Grade*

Solve the following word problems.

1. If it is 8:05 a.m. now, what time will it be in four hours?

_____

2. Chizuko went to sleep at 9 p.m. and woke up at 7 a.m. How long did she sleep?

_____

3. If a loaf of bread costs $1.25 and milk costs $2.50, how much do they cost together?

_____

4. Pierre has a dollar. He buys a toy that costs 69 cents. How much change does he get?

_____

5. Sonya earns $5.25 per hour. If she works for six hours, how much does she earn?

_____

0 to 1 **✗**, put a check in the chart on page 65 and go to the next page. 2 or more **✗** s, stop here and review skills; retest at a later date.

Graphs
Third Grade

Based on the graph, answer the following questions.

Height Chart

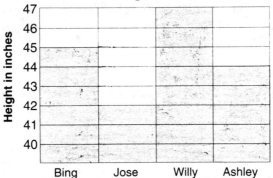

1. Which child is the tallest?

2. Which child is the shortest?

3. How much taller is Bing than Ashley?

4. How tall is Bing?

5. If all the children stood on top of each other, how tall would they be?

0 to 1 ✗, put a check in the chart on page 65 and go to the next page. 2 or more ✗s, stop here and review skills; retest at a later date.

Division with Remainders   *Third Grade*

Solve the following division problems.

1. $3\overline{)11}$ 6. $2\overline{)21}$

2. $5\overline{)36}$ 7. $9\overline{)40}$

3. $7\overline{)48}$ 8. $5\overline{)68}$

4. $8\overline{)100}$ 9. $6\overline{)50}$

5. $4\overline{)51}$ 10. $9\overline{)12}$

0 to 2 ✗ s, put a check in the chart on page 65 and go to the next page. 3 or more ✗ s, stop here and review skills; retest at a later date.

Mixed Word Problems

Third Grade

Read the following questions and check the correct answer.

1. If 8 children each have 4 toys each, how many toys do they have in all?

    _____

2. If a cake is cut into 9 pieces, and there are 3 children, how many pieces does each child get?

    _____

3. If Mario had four bags of marbles and each bag held sixteen marbles, how many marbles did he have in all?

    _____

4. If there are 32 children in a class and there are 8 rows, how many children were in each row?

    _____

5. Write the following words in number form:
    Five hundred sixty five thousand two hundred seventy four

    _____

0 to 1 ✖, put a check in the chart on page 65 and go to the next page. 2 or more ✖s, stop here and review skills; retest at a later date.

Rounding Off & Estimating   *Fourth Grade*

Round off each number to the nearest 10:

1. 42 _____   2. 26 _____

Round off each number to the nearest 100:

3. 119 _____   4. 462 _____

Estimate

5. 10 feet is approximately how many yards?

    _____

6. 23 inches is approximately how many feet?

    _____

7. 125 days is approximately how many months?

    _____

Average

8. Hector is 3 feet tall. Jamaal is 4 feet tall. Yuzi is 5 feet tall. What is the average height?

    _____

9. The soccer team took the following days off: 6 in January; 3 in February; 4 in March; 7 in April. What is the monthly average?

    _____

10. Luis has $10 to spend per day on a four-day trip. His trip took five days instead of four. How much is his daily allowance for the five days?

    _____

---

0 to 2 ✘ s, put a check in the chart on page 65 and go to the next page. 3 or more ✘ s, stop here and review skills; retest at a later date.

Multiple Digit Computing   *Fourth Grade*

Solve the following problems.

1.   13   6.   75 $\overline{)425}$
     x 32

2.   43   7.   53 $\overline{)\$6.89}$
     x 61

3.   27   8.   71 $\overline{)\$4.97}$
     x 39

4.   56   9.   58 $\overline{)291}$
     x 65

5.   35   10.   90 $\overline{)400}$
     x 65

---

0 to 2 ✖ s, put a check in the chart on page 65 and go to the next page. 3 or more ✖ s, stop here and review skills; retest at a later date.

Computing with Fractions   *Fourth Grade*

Reduce each fraction to its lowest terms.

1. $\dfrac{2}{4}$ 2. $\dfrac{8}{24}$ 3. $\dfrac{75}{100}$

Compare using >, <, = .

4. $\dfrac{2}{4}$ $\dfrac{1}{4}$ 5. $\dfrac{5}{6}$ $\dfrac{1}{2}$ 6. $\dfrac{1}{3}$ $\dfrac{3}{9}$

Reduce and write a mixed number or a whole number.

7. $\dfrac{4}{4}$ 8. $\dfrac{20}{5}$

9. $\dfrac{9}{2}$ 10. $\dfrac{11}{6}$

Add or subtract these fractions and reduce to lowest terms.

11.   3/4 + 3/4 =   12.   4 1/4 + 2 3/4 =

13.   7/8 – 5/8 =   14.   1 3/6 + 3 4/12 =

> 0 to 3 ✘s, put a check in the chart on page 65 and go to the
> next page. 4 or more ✘s, stop here and review skills; retest
> at a later date.

Measurements

Fourth Grade

Read the following questions and mark the correct answer.

1. If there are 10 kids playing and they need drinks, about how much juice would be needed for them altogether?

   ❏ a pint   ❏ a quart   ❏ a gallon

2. If there are 10 millimeters in a centimeter and 100 centimeters in a meter, how many millimeters are in a meter? _____

3. To measure the distance between your eyes, which unit of measurement should be used?

   ❏ mm   ❏ cm   ❏ m   ❏ km

4. To measure how far a person can walk in 1 hour, which unit of measurement should be used?

   ❏ mm   ❏ cm   ❏ m   ❏ km

5. Compare using > or <.

   16 feet _____ 6 yards

---

0 to 1 ✗, put a check in the chart on page 65 and go to the next page. 2 or more ✗s, stop here and review skills; retest at a later date.

Mixed Word Problems
Fourth Grade

Read the following questions and check the correct answer.

1. What is the chance of drawing a red marble from a bowl that has one red, one blue and one green marble?
   ❏ even   ❏ 1 in 2   ❏ 1 in 3

2. An oak tree is 50 feet tall. If it can grow three times that height, how tall can it grow?
   ❏ 50 feet   ❏ 150 feet   ❏ 300 feet

3. 37 children are going in vans to Disneyland. Each van seats 8 children. How many vans are needed?
   ❏ 4 vans   ❏ 5 vans   ❏ 6 vans

4. Ali spent one third of his money for lunch, and he gave one sixth of it to his brother. How much did he have left?
   ❏ 1/6   ❏ 1/3   ❏ 1/2

5. Twelve children are at a party. Half of the children are drinking punch and half of those children are also eating popcorn. How many children are having both popcorn and punch?
   ❏ four   ❏ six   ❏ three

0 to 1 ✖, put a check in the chart on page 65 and go to the next page. 2 or more ✖s, stop here and review skills; retest at a later date.

Multiplying & Dividing Fractions   *Fifth Grade*

Multiply or divide these fractions. Reduce if necessary.

1. 3/4   x   4/3   =

2. 2/5   x   3/5   =

3. 3/9   x   3/9   =

4. 2/2   x   4/12   =

5. 1/4   x   3   =

6. 1/3   ÷   1/4   =

7. 2/3   ÷   4/5   =

8. 5/8   ÷   3/4   =

9. 7/10   ÷   1/10   =

10. 2/5   ÷   1/3   =

0 to 2 ✘ s, put a check in the chart on page 65 and go to the next page. 3 or more ✘ s, stop here and review skills; retest at a later date.

Graphs

Fifth Grade

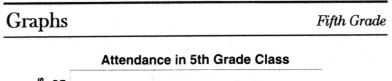

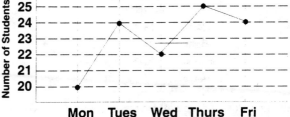

Attendance in 5th Grade Class

1. How many students were at school on Tuesday?

   _____

2. How many more students were in school on Thursday than on Monday?

   _____

3. What is the average attendance for the week?

   _____

4. What fraction of the day is used by Math and PE?
   ❏ 1/8   ❏ 1/4   ❏ 1/2   ❏ 1   ❏ 2   ❏ 4

5. How much more of the day is used by Science than PE?
   ❏ 1/8   ❏ 1/4   ❏ 1/2   ❏ 1   ❏ 2   ❏ 4

> 0 to 1 ✖, put a check in the chart on page 65 and go to the next page. 2 or more ✖ s, stop here and review skills; retest at a later date.

Tables

5th Grade Bike-a-thon

	No. of Miles
Lina	𝍷𝍷𝍷𝍷𝍷 𝍷𝍷
Brian	𝍷𝍷𝍷𝍷
Miguel	𝍷𝍷𝍷𝍷𝍷 𝍷𝍷𝍷𝍷𝍷
Helga	𝍷𝍷𝍷𝍷𝍷 𝍷

1. How many miles did all the children ride in all?

   _____

2. If Lina received 50 cents for every mile she rode, how much money did she bring in?

   _____

3. What is the average number of miles ridden?

   _____

	# of Days		# of Days
January	31	July	31
February	28	August	31
March	31	September	30
April	30	October	31
May	31	November	30
June	30	December	31

4. If today is August 1, how many more days until Christmas (December 25)?

   _____

5. What is the average number of days in a month?

   _____

0 to 1 ✗, put a check in the chart on page 65 and go to the next page. 2 or more ✗ s, stop here and review skills; retest at a later date.

Measurements   *Fifth Grade*

Use the centimeter side of your ruler to make the following measurements to the *nearest centimeter*.

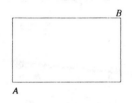

1. What is the length in centimeters of one of the longer sides of the rectangle?_____

2. What is the length in centimeters of the diagonal from A to B?_____

3. On the grid below, draw a rectangle with an area of 12 square units.

4. How many pints equal one gallon?
   ❑ 4   ❑ 8   ❑ 12

5. How many quarts of water are in a 5 gallon jug?
   ❑ 16   ❑ 20   ❑ 40

0 to 1 ✖, put a check in the chart on page 65 and go to the next page. 2 or more ✖ s, stop here and review skills; retest at a later date.

Geometry

Fifth Grade

1. What is the perimeter of this polygon?

_____

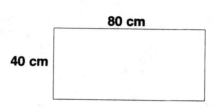

2. What is the perimeter of an octagon where each size measures two inches?

_____

3. How many faces does a cube have?

_____

4. Which of the following is a right angle? Circle your answer.

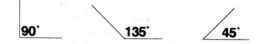

5. Which two letters represent the radius of the circle?

   ❑ B C

   ❑ B D

   ❑ A C

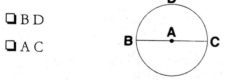

0 to 1 ✖, put a check in the chart on page 65 and go to the next page. 2 or more ✖ s, stop here and review skills; retest at a later date.

Fractions & Decimals   *Fifth Grade*

Write the decimal or fraction for each problem.

1. $\dfrac{3}{5}$ _____

2. .40   _____

3. $\dfrac{1}{4}$ _____

Solve the following decimal problems.

4. .5 + .25 =   _____

5. .75 − .25 =   _____

Write the following as percentages.

6. 7/10   _____

7. 4/5   _____

8. 2/8   _____

9. 11/20   _____

10. .78   _____

0 to 2 **✗** s, put a check in the chart on page 65 and go to the next page. 3 or more **✗** s, stop here and review skills; retest at a later date.

Word Problems   *Fifth Grade*

Read the following questions and check the correct answer.

1. It took Chelsea 2 hours and 15 minutes to fill out 45 forms. What was the average time spent on each form?

    _____

2. 16 children collected rocks along the beach, finding a total of 48 rocks. What was the average number of rocks found per child?

    _____

3. Quincey bought four lobsters for $3 a pound. They weighed 13 oz., 14 oz., 17 oz., and 20 oz. How much did she spend?

    _____

4. If it is now 11:45 a.m., what time will it be in 20 minutes?

    _____

5. Twenty people are swimming in a pool. Another 16 join them, but the pool becomes crowded and 9 people have to leave. What fraction of the people had to leave?

    _____

0 to 1 ✗, put a check in the **chart on page 65** and go to the next page. 2 or more ✗s, stop here and review skills; retest at a later date.

Progress Chart

In these tests, the goal is for your child to succeed at a minimum of 80 percent accuracy. As you give each test, check the bottom of the page for the allowable number of errors, which will depend on the number of items in the section. If your child completes a test at 80 percent accuracy or better, enter the date the test was passed on this chart.

Level	Topic	Passed
Kindergarten	Shapes & sizes	
	Patterns & counting	
	Recognizing numbers 1-10	
	Writing numbers 1-10	
1st Grade	Recognizing numbers 1-100	
	Writing numbers 1-100	
	Signs & skip counting	
	Sequencing & ordering	
	Single & double digit addition	
	Single & double digit subtraction	
	Time & money	
	Patterns	

Level	Topic	Passed
2nd Grade	Time & money	
	Computation with regrouping	
	Simple fractions	
	3 digit mixed computation	
	Word problems	
3rd Grade	Single digit multiplication/division	
	Double digit multiplication/division	
	Time & money	
	Graphs	
	Division with remainders	
	Mixed word problems	
4th Grade	Rounding off & estimating	
	Multiple digit computing	
	Computing with fractions	
	Measurements	
	Mixed Word problems	
5th Grade	Multiplying & dividing fractions	
	Graphs	
	Tables	
	Measurements	
	Geometry	
	Fractions & decimals	
	Mixed word problems	

Grade Level Guidelines

I love math!

Starting point

The first things a parent of a child just beginning to learn math wants to know are: Where do we start? What comes first? What is important?!

The main problem with parents teaching math is that they don't realize how much time and repetition is involved in cementing the basics of arithmetic in a child's mind.

For children, math (learning the numbers, putting them in the right order, printing them neatly and correctly, knowing the function and understanding the computation) is like trying to see the forest for the trees. Each element may be clear, but putting them all together for the big picture is extremely difficult. Months of flash cards, pages of sums, and hours of practicing are necessary to make those facts and relationships clear in a child's memory and fully at hand to be recalled instantly.

Fortunately, math is a step-by-step, cumulative system. There is a comfortable sequence for children to follow in learning arithmetic, leading naturally into higher math.

In terms of working with your own child, however, it is crucial to remember that there are stages of learning, types of memory, ways of learning, and internal time frames in which children learn. In general, children learn by doing. They are more successful with hands-on, colorful, concrete exercises, instead of more abstract, black-and-white, pencil-and-paper exercises. For example, having a child rearrange number cards to manipulate sums will make a stronger, more lasting impression than if she just sits and looks at numbers on a page. Children will easily learn the pre-basics of math from manipulation—the handling and moving around of blocks, coins, or pieces of fruit. In time, with gentle encouragement, they will start to make the connection between numbers printed on the page, the physical realities, and the abstract concepts.

There are two general techniques that work well in finding out what is going on with a child's math skills. First, check what *type* of error was made. For instance, if a child carries the wrong number, this would require different practice from a child who lined up the numbers wrong.

The other technique is to ask the child to say what she is thinking and doing *while* she is doing the problem. When the words stop making sense, then the parent can step in to assist. Some children have a more purely intuitive sense of math, though, and would have great difficulty articulating the thought process, so like everything, this is a process of trial and error.

Each grade level in this section lays out the typical types of mistakes for that particular range. Of course, there will be some overlap from grade to grade, because the skills are cumulative.

Math should be fun, not work

There will be a wide range in ability, interest, and performance among children. It may extend from an engaged interest to complete detachment and disinterest in numbers and counting. Some children make the connection between the objects or pictures (△△△), the spoken number *(three bells)*, and the printed numeral (**3**) at an earlier age than others. To a small child, there is not much difference between drawing six bells and counting six bells, so incorporate objects as well as pictures and numbers into your play time.

Math *is* serious, but 5-year-olds need to be taught playfully. Play counting games and sing counting songs. Have the child count the place settings as he sets the table, or count the number of knobs in the kitchen. This will help lay the foundation for understanding sequencing and order.

Stay calm

Parents are well aware of the importance of arithmetic and the enormous effect it will have on a child's future. All parents want their children to understand math, and to use it well and often. These days especially, with television such an omnipresent attraction, the official window of opportunity—the 2nd and 3rd grades—for children to start becoming numerate can be a worrisome period for parents.

Hovering anxiously over children while they pick through their numbers, stumble over "easy" sums, and write large, messy numbers, a parent may become frustrated. Sometimes kids like to tease their parents. They may pretend to forget large amounts of information (*Dad! What's six plus two again?*). If you feel yourself getting upset (*But you **know** the answer to this!* or *We've been **over** this!* or *We're going to sit here until you finish!*), it's time to back off and make a fresh start later.

There are not many guarantees in life, but if you sit patiently night after night, playing with flash cards, explaining the rules of math to your child, reinforcing this understanding with her own experiences, and finally, pointing out where you use math everyday, you will have a child who is good at arithmetic. If you go through these steps, you will achieve 100 percent numeracy in your home.

Arithmetic is an enjoyable activity, not a punishment, and it should be taught playfully and lovingly. It is extremely important to keep it positive so that your child won't be permanently put off by math. One day, it will all make sense to her. Your job, as a parent, is to keep practicing the fundamentals until that day comes.

So, stay calm, and turn off the TV.

Kindergarten

Basic skills

Most kindergartners should know how to count up to 15 or 20 objects and recognize numbers up to 20. Some may know how to print 0 to 9, but this depends on their fine motor skills. Importantly, children need to know that there are *numbers* and an association between each number and its amount (three = **3** = △△△).

In texts appropriate for kindergartners, there should be a picture for every number so that they can *see* the idea.

A 5- or 6-year-old should recognize the basic shapes: circle, square, triangle. Children should know the names and be able to point each one out from a group of shapes.

Circle   Square   Triangle

They should know the positions—right, left, top, and bottom—so they can put their names on their papers in the proper position, they can count numbers from right to left and top to bottom, and can open the math book at the front, rather than the back.

Once a child is comfortable with counting, he needs to be able to start putting amounts together: adding. Adults tend to take addition for granted. Children need to have it reinforced. Start with concrete information. Ask your child, *"If you and Bobby were playing ball, how many kids would that be? Then if Billy and Sue came, how many would there be?"* She will naturally know the answer. But having to stop, think about it, and explain it will help develop simple addition. As a parent and adult, you have to recognize that concepts that you take for granted need to be pointed out to children with concrete examples.

Kindergartners are now ready for more games and songs. Songs that work well are some of the old standards such as "One Potato, Two Potato"; "There Were 10 in the Bed" (this teaches counting backwards which is helpful for subtraction). Counting games, such as dominoes, help a child count "for a reason."

A further support for your child's arithmetic skill building is the use of flash cards. Flash cards are helpful for visual learners.

Start with counting cards that have pictures on them and work up to recognizing the numbers and then simple addition.

Common difficulties

1. **Number discrimination**
   Children have to learn to recognize the visual configurations of a given number. When they are learning the ABCs and 0 to 9, kindergartners who are having trouble may either not know how to write a number or may confuse it with a letter, such as **9** and **p** or **9** and **q**. When practicing with the child, it is helpful to keep numbers and letters separate until the distinction is made. Have the child find and circle the same numbers from a list of similar ones.

2	6	8	2	9

This helps a child recognize the visual shape of the number and compare it with the others.

2. **Sequencing**

   Adults know that there is sequential order in counting, but in the beginning, children are perfectly happy to say 1–2–3–7–5–9–6–10! Proper sequencing is simply a matter of engraining the order in a child's mind with number songs, counting stories and number games. Fill-in-the-blank exercises give a child practice in sequencing and writing. He *says* the numbers, *thinks about* the number that comes next, and *writes* the missing number in the box.

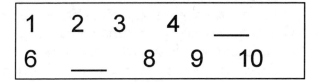

   When you are helping a kindergartner with this type of exercise, cover up everything except the row you are working on. The whole exercise may look too "busy" to a child's eye.

3. **Math concepts**

   Objects are concrete and real, numbers are abstract and intangible. An association between a *number* and an *amount* of things must be formed. For example, put four apples on a table and talk to your child about the number **4**. Sesame Street videos are excellent for counting and numbers.

4. **Fine motor coordination**

   Fine motor skills for writing numbers are
   generally lacking in 5-year-old fingers. Have
   your child trace numbers to develop an
   understanding of the shapes involved and the
   order of the stroke (top to bottom). Practicing
   drawing little circles and sticks is easy and
   fun for a child. Combining the circles and
   sticks for numbers allows the child to see the
   basic shapes and combinations, while
   memorizing the nine digits.

5. **Math vocabulary**

   In this first year of school, a child's
   vocabulary increases to include specific
   "school words." Part of this is the language of
   math and the vocabulary of spatial concepts.
   Children need to understand verbal
   meanings of words such as *under, over, more,
   less,* and *between* in order to follow directions
   in the math lessons.

More kindergarten skills

◆ **Counting**

   Counting starts in kindergarten and
   kindergartners need to know how to count
   from 0 to 9. Counting simple groups of objects
   and writing the answers in number form
   allows a child to understand the correlation
   between a number of objects and the written
   number.

A good way to practice is by having your child put dots in boxes. They are neat and easy to keep track of. Have your child practice writing the correct number:

What number is shown in each box?

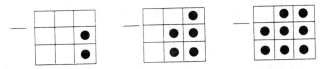

...as well as putting the correct number of dots in the boxes:

Draw the correct number of dots in each box.

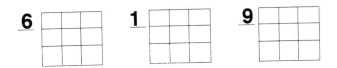

♦ **Shape recognition**
The three shapes that are introduced first are the circle, the square, and the triangle. Have your child find and color the same shape from a list of similar ones.

This exercise helps a child recognize visual shapes and compare them with the others.

Parents can help a child identify these three shapes by pointing out the characteristics:

 A square has 4 equal sides and 4 corners;

O A circle is round;

△ A triangle has 3 sides and 3 corners.

In order to familiarize a child with these shapes, call the shapes by their names and use them in drawing, so a child can see, for example, that a house or a person can be made with these shapes.

First Grade

Basic skills

Simple addition and subtraction should be mastered in the 1st grade. First graders should be able to count up to 100, and be completely familiar with basic addition and subtraction facts up to $9 + 9 = 18$ and $9 - 9 = 0$. They should be able to figure out simple addition word problems. They should know the coins and denominations and be able to add up to a dollar.

By the end of 1st grade, students should be familiar with the *mechanics* of arithmetic—the rules of addition, such as the commutative rule. For example, $1 + 2 = 3$ and $2 + 1 = 3$ have the same answer, even though the digits being added are in a different order. When explaining this number concept to a child, it's essential for him to visualize the problem:

$$\bullet + \bullet\bullet = \bullet\bullet\bullet \text{ and } \bullet\bullet + \bullet = \bullet\bullet\bullet$$

First graders should be able to count by 2s, 5s, and 10s and should know the easy way to add 9s (see pages page 95-96).

It is not unusual to see a child still counting on his fingers at this stage, but memorization is the preferred way to learn math facts. While finger counting is not a cause for worry, it should be used only if a child has a specific memory recall deficit. For a child who has trouble memorizing things, it is better to have finger counting as a backup than to simply start randomly guessing answers. If you suspect that there is a specific difficulty—whether it is a behavioral problem or a learning disability—do not hesitate to discuss this with the school principal, teacher, or school psychologist. Hearing and vision should also be checked.

A 1st grader should know that when you put two numbers together, they make certain bigger numbers but not others (**2 + 4 = 6** and not **2 + 4 = 24**).

Being able to find the small sum within a bigger problem is a great advantage in early math. For example, **23 + 23** is a *big* number to a 1st grader, but **2 + 2** and **3 + 3** can be easily figured out. So by learning the basic skills, a child will be ready to grasp more advanced skills that follow.

A child can have fairly good addition skills, but have great difficulty with subtraction. Therefore, subtraction should not be started until addition is second nature.

Familiarity with the **number families** will help a child understand the relationship between addition and subtraction. Subtraction is the *reverse* of addition. It is important for children to see and understand this relationship. Manipulatives (blocks, coins, etc.) help a child see that *subtracting 3* is just the opposite of *adding 3*. If a child can count backwards, it will help him understand subtraction.

The math vocabulary of addition and subtraction needs to be explained. You can correlate familiar words with the new terms your child is learning. **Addition** means **putting together** and can also be called **adding** or **plus**. Other addition words are **more than**, **increased,** and so on. **Subtraction** means **taking away** and can also be called **minus**, **subtract**, and **take away**. Other subtraction words are **less than** and **fewer than**.

When a child doesn't understand the relationship between *-teen* and *ten*, it can impede simple addition. "Teen" and "ten" are the same thing. Six*teen* is really *six-ten*, or six plus ten, so when a child is adding a number between 3 and 9 to *ten*, he just needs to think *-teen*.

Trouble with addition can also be caused by a sequencing difficulty. Before a young child memorizes a math fact, such as **8 plus 5 equals 13**, he starts counting—or sequencing—from 8 and adds on another 5. If he has trouble sequencing, this will show up in his having trouble with days of the week, putting things in order, prioritizing, and even in social situations where appropriate behavior follows certain sequential patterns. If you notice that your child has trouble sequencing, focus him on tasks that help him prioritize.

In addition to numbers and patterns, 1st graders refine some distinctions among shapes. Kindergartners learn the three basic shapes: *circle, square,* and *triangle*; 1st graders add on variations of those with *oval, rectangle,* and *pentagon.* If these are not making sense spatially, it helps to use words to clarify, such as *round* for a circle and *egg-shaped* for oval. The difference between a *square* and a *rectangle* is not immediately obvious, so the parent can point out that a rectangle has two opposite sides that are longer, while a square has four *equal* sides. *Pentagons* are five-sided and stop signs are *octagons* (eight-sided).

Another form of numbers, patterns, shapes, and counting is money. First graders need to understand the relationship of coins to value. If a parent has ever traveled to another country where different coins are used, he will empathize with how difficult it is to associate an actual amount with a little round piece of metal—and then to quickly add them together in order to buy something! Children need to learn which number is represented by which coin and, conversely, how much each coin is worth (a nickel is 5 cents, a dime is 10 cents, etc., but there is no "7 cent coin").

Common difficulties

1. **Math signs**
   Confusion between **addition** and
   subtraction is common. While a 1st grader
   should know both functions, he may forget to
   look for the sign. You might see either a total
   disregard for the sign—adding when it's
   easier and subtracting when it's easier—or
   perhaps adding no matter what the sign.
   Before starting each problem, have the child
   circle the sign and say *plus* or *minus*.

2. **Illegible numbers**
   Boys generally have good large motor skills,
   but often have trouble with their fine motor
   skills. The consequence of this is messy
   writing of numbers and math problems,
   which can either cause a wrong answer or be
   read as a wrong answer. If this is the case
   with your child, get out the graph paper and
   have him write one number per grid box. This
   will confine his numbers as well as align his
   sums.

3. **Faulty memory**
   When a child forgets sums he knows well,
   there could be a variety of factors at play.
   Perhaps it has been a long time since he used
   the skill and he is rusty. Perhaps he is in the
   process of acquiring a new skill such as
   multiplication, which in the short run, can
   cause lapses in addition, or perhaps he has
   poor memory recall. It could also be that as he

sees math getting progressively more difficult, he chooses to rest at a comfortable spot for a while as he gears up for the more difficult problems ahead. In this situation, go back to the basics. Review, starting from a level where he has 100 percent mastery and gradually add higher level work.

More 1st grade skills

♦ **Vertical sums vs. horizontal sums**
One of the fascinating aspects of math is that it is a language—a *symbol language*. This will become apparent at two early stages. The first place the symbols come into play is when you switch from vertical sums to horizontal sums:

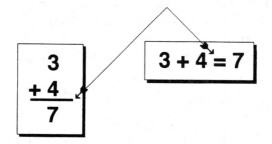

These are two different symbols representing **equals**. Children need to practice both vertical and horizontal sums until they are equally easy.

♦ Counting and adding

First graders need to solidify their understanding of amounts and the numbers that represent those amounts. Exercises in which the child counts objects and writes the numbers help make the connections for him. For 6-year-olds, make sure that the pictures are large and easy to count.

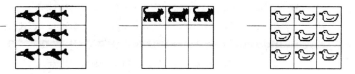

How many planes, cats, and ducks are there?

Practice making groups of dots to be added together. Allow your child to use colored markers so that the groups of dots can be distinguished. This is a good way to explain how to add two amounts.

♦ Writing numbers

A 1st grader should be able to write each number in order from 1 to 100. Use lined paper to form a grid and have your child practice writing the numbers if he is not yet proficient in doing so.

♦ Number families

First graders should know that for each equation and its inverse equation (for example, addition and its inverse, subtraction), there are number families.

These are made of three numbers that will be used in four different equations. Use the following steps to teach this concept to your child.

Step 1: Introduce the three numbers you will be using (in this case 1, 2, 3).

Step 2: Have your child use the three numbers to make four different equations. This exercise is first written and then read aloud. Have your child focus not only on the *order* of the numbers, but on the *signs*.

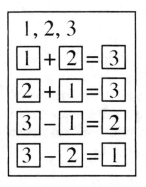

♦ **Groups of five**
A 1st grader should learn the concept of a group of five, so he doesn't have to start from 1 each time he adds. He can start with 5, and then say "6, 7...". This concept of counting groups rather than individual units will hold a child in good stead for more advanced addition and multiplication. Use a group of objects, such as raisins, to practice the concept of a group of five with your child. For example, group five raisins together and work

with your child to show him how one more makes six, two more make seven, and so on.

♦ **More than (>), less than (<), equal to (=)**
A 1st grader should have enough of a grasp of the relationship between numbers to understand the quantity a number represents. This can then be applied to comparing numbers to determine *more* and *less*. In math symbols, *more* is represented by > and *less* is represented by <. A helpful hint is that the bigger side of the shape is next to the bigger number, and the smaller side is by the smaller number. Therefore, you would write **24 > 7** or **7 < 24**. If the numbers being compared are equal, the symbol is =.

♦ **Using flash cards**
Flash cards aid in memory recall and discourage finger counting. At the 1st grade level, 10 minutes of review per day is sufficient to drill the sums from **1 + 1** to **10 + 10**. Repetition is the soul of learning, and the more reinforcement of the basics that a child has, the better he will do at every subsequent level in math.

In the beginning, have your child write the problem *and the answer* on the card. Participation will encourage a child to use the cards, the actual writing will be a memory aid, and the visual reinforcement of saying and *seeing* the sum is important. After your child demonstrates a facility for reading the sums and answers, move on to sumless cards.

Second Grade

Basic skills

Second graders should have the basic addition and subtraction skills down cold. Simple sums should be second nature and the child should start adding longer and longer problems, rather than just one digit to one digit.

Consistency is important. Every child should sit and do computation for 15 minutes a day. She can be with the parent or on her own, doing flash cards with a parent or a sibling or silently to herself. Choosing the function herself (addition or subtraction) will give a child greater incentive to practice. Although the level may seem too easy to you, or it may seem that she has gone through the cards so many times, let her choose the function for the 15-minute drills. As the parent, your job is to make certain that your child sits still and practices. This means checking to make sure that her answers are correct. Encourage her to ask for help and discourage her from counting on her fingers.

After adding and subtracting, a child starts working with more difficult word problems. This is where her math vocabulary will start expanding to include real-life situations in word problems, with people joining and leaving groups, eating portions of pizza, and sharing toys.

Second graders can run into difficulty with sequencing because they are using both larger numbers and larger increments of skip counting.

By the end of the 2nd grade, a child should understand the concepts of "parts" and "a whole." This is the basis of fractions. A fraction is part of a whole. The most simple and common is 1/2, which is 1 part of 2 parts of a whole.

One half can be illustrated with any variety of regular and irregular shapes:

For computational purposes, 1st graders generally become familiar with the front of coins, because there are clearly different heads and faces there. Second graders need to start recognizing the backs of coins, as well as be able to identify them by size and color.

Second graders should be able to count by 5s very well, so this leads naturally into using a clock, which is in increments of five. As a child tells time, she is automatically practicing counting by 5s, which in turn leads into multiplication. For example, if the little hand is on the **12** and the big hand is on the **4**, she skip counts up to 20, for 12:20, or multiplies **4 x 5** for the same result.

Common difficulties

1. **Math signs**
   Confusion between addition and subtraction is still common at the 2nd-grade level.

Although these are 1st grade skills, 2nd graders can get caught up in the harder numbers or regrouping, and forget to look for the sign. If this is a consistent problem, have your child resume the habit of circling the sign and saying the words *plus* or *minus* to refocus attention.

2. Misalignment and errors in place values

A 2nd grader needs to understand that each *column* has a place value. This will ease her understanding of adding numbers (as well as the other functions). Often poor alignment will cause the wrong numbers to be computed. For children who consistently misalign, graph paper is an excellent way to line up columns of numbers.

3. Confusion in regrouping

Particularly with problems involving regrouping, children can get confused about what stays and what gets carried. Often, a child will have a sum such as 13, but write down the 1 and carry the 3. If you see this problem occurring, it means the child does not understand place notation. Ask her which number is in the ones column and which is in the tens. If she responds correctly, work with her concentration and attention to detail. If she responds incorrectly, work on place notation. Do exercises like these:

Circle the number

in the tens column: **452**
in the ones column: **429**
in the hundreds column: **672**

4. **Random guesses**
   Sometimes a child may just make a wild
   guess and put down random numbers. This
   would indicate that she needed more work at
   the previous level. In this case, spend time
   reviewing skills previously learned.

5. **Illegible numbers**
   If a child has poor motor coordination or tries
   to write too fast, the resulting numbers will
   be difficult or impossible to read. Children
   usually write sentences before they do sums,
   and it is possible to figure out one poorly
   shaped letter from context. Children need to
   know that this is *not* true of math. The parent
   should spend time with the child practicing
   writing the numbers 0 through 9.

More 2nd grade skills

♦ **Math vocabulary**
   Math vocabulary is a major factor in
   converting word problems to number
   problems.

*It took **15** minutes to get dressed <u>and</u> **5** minutes to eat breakfast. How long did it take to get ready <u>all together</u>?*

The key to word problems is to take them step by step. After the child reads the problem, first have her pick out the numbers: **15** and **5**. With addition, there is no "right order," as there is with subtraction, but in order to get ready for subtraction, have her put the larger number on top.

15 minutes to get dressed

5 minutes to eat

The next step is deciding on the sign. Go over the problem again, and find the word that would indicate addition or subtraction—*and, plus, with, more, all together* are addition words; *took out, lost, left behind, forgot* are subtraction words.

15 minutes

+ 5 minutes

20 minutes all together

♦ **Tens complements**
Each number has a set of combinations that when added together equal that number. These are called *complements.*

0	+	10	=	10
1	+	9	=	10
2	+	8	=	10
3	+	7	=	10
4	+	6	=	10
5	+	5	=	10
6	+	4	=	10
7	+	3	=	10
8	+	2	=	10
9	+	1	=	10
10	+	0	=	10

The *tens complements* indicate when it's time to carry, because whenever the total from a column is more than 10, anything over 10 stays in that column and the whole 10 is carried over to the next column. For example, if in a column you are adding 7 and 6, the tens complement would be 7 and 3, leaving an extra 3. So the 3 would stay in that column, and the whole 10 (written as 1) would be carried to the next column.

♦ **Adding 10 to a number**
Adding 10 to a number is very easy. Drop off the **zero** from the **10**, and replace it with the number you are adding.

10 +	**0**	**=**	**10**	"teen"
10 +	**1**	**=**	**11**	"oneteen"
10 +	**2**	**=**	**12**	"twoteen"
10 +	**3**	**=**	**13**	thirteen
10 +	**4**	**=**	**14**	fourteen
10 +	**5**	**=**	**15**	fifteen
10 +	**6**	**=**	**16**	sixteen
10 +	**7**	**=**	**17**	seventeen
10 +	**8**	**=**	**18**	eighteen
10 +	**9**	**=**	**19**	nineteen
10+	**10**	**=**	**20**	twenty

For children, the distinction between a *number* and a *digit* helps clarify place notation. They can think of the whole number as being made up of digits in the ones column, tens column, and so on. **10** is a number, made up of two digits (**1** in the tens column and **0** in the ones column).When adding a number from 1 to 9 to a ten, the number being added goes in the ones column, in place of the zero.

♦ **Adding 9 to a number**
Adding with 9 is just like adding with 10, but one number smaller—that is, add 10 and subtract 1. You can think of it as:

9	=	10 − 1
9 + 9	=	10 + 10 − 2
9 + 9 + 9	=	10 + 10 + 10 − 3

◆ **Number families**

As was introduced in the 1st grade, for every group of three numbers, there are four problems—two addition and two subtraction. Here we will use **7, 8,** and **15**.

$$7 + 8 = 15$$
$$8 + 7 = 15$$
$$15 - 8 = 7$$
$$15 - 7 = 8$$

A child should be able to quickly recognize and recall these number families along with the individual computations. Fill-in-the-blank exercises use skills that are effective for both addition and subtraction:

$$7 + \underline{} = 15$$
$$15 - \underline{} = 7$$

Here are some of the common but difficult combinations that need to be practiced a lot. Make cards and put them up around the house. Choose one group per day and work on it. Don't mix groups until each one is mastered.

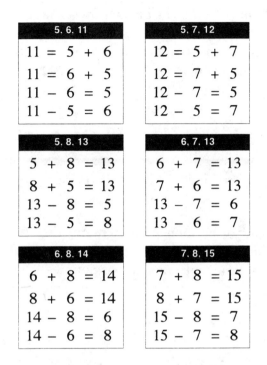

5, 6, 11
11 = 5 + 6
11 = 6 + 5
11 − 6 = 5
11 − 5 = 6

5, 7, 12
12 = 5 + 7
12 = 7 + 5
12 − 7 = 5
12 − 5 = 7

5, 8, 13
5 + 8 = 13
8 + 5 = 13
13 − 8 = 5
13 − 5 = 8

6, 7, 13
6 + 7 = 13
7 + 6 = 13
13 − 7 = 6
13 − 6 = 7

6, 8, 14
6 + 8 = 14
8 + 6 = 14
14 − 8 = 6
14 − 6 = 8

7, 8, 15
7 + 8 = 15
8 + 7 = 15
15 − 8 = 7
15 − 7 = 8

♦ **Addition and carrying**
In addition, when the ones column is full, we need to start filling up the tens column. To many children, it seems that, in carrying, the number has to *jump* over to another column.

9

+ 1

10

The question is, how do you add these two groups together, and how do the numbers in the *ones column* jump over to the *tens column?* Using the grids below, imagine that the dots are pennies, as **10 pennies = 1 dime** is an easy concept for 2nd graders. As the child can see, there's just no room in the box for that 10th penny.

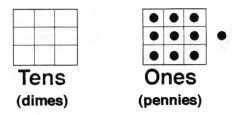

Tens
(dimes)

Ones
(pennies)

So, what happens? All 10 penny dots need to *move over* to the left and turn into one shiny new dime, with no leftover pennies.

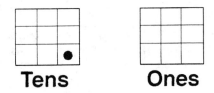

Tens

Ones

What happens if you want to add other numbers? It's the same process—let's try **6 + 6**.

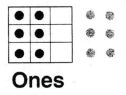

Ones

Of course, all six of the new dots won't fit into the ones box with the six that are already there, so 10 of those dots form one ten, and the remaining dots (2) are the ones.

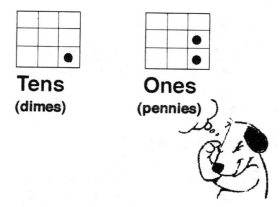

Tens
(dimes)

Ones
(pennies)

♦ **Borrowing**
Subtraction is just the inverse of addition. With addition, the question is, "Where do we carry to?" With subtraction, the question is, "Where do we borrow from?" And both times in double digit addition, the answer is the *tens column.* (As children get into three-or-more digit addition and subtraction, they can apply this rule to carrying to or borrowing from the hundreds column, the thousands column, and so on.) Let's start with **46:**

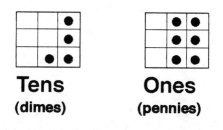

Tens
(dimes)

Ones
(pennies)

Then we are going to subtract **9**. One **10** decompresses itself back into 10 temporary **ones**:

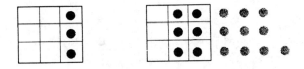

Remove 9 of the **ones** dots:

And you are left with 37:

Third Grade

Basic skills

Math starts to accelerate in the 3rd grade. Children do larger and more complicated addition and subtraction problems, with regrouping (carrying and borrowing).

$$4396 \quad 7891$$
$$+ \; 2844 \quad - \; 2908$$

Strong basics are extremely important at this level. Arithmetic is strictly sequential, with addition being a fundamental component of multiplication, and subtraction being the inverse of addition. Addition and subtraction skills must be stimulus/response—with no hesitation whatsoever. The multiplication facts also need to be similarly memorized.

Third graders are expected to be accurate in the use of greater than (>) and less than (<) signs. They should be able to identify fractions of a whole number, such as **1/2 of 10** is **5**. They are becoming familiar with the concepts of decimal values such as tenths and hundredths—using money to represent these values.

Children learn that multiplication is a shortcut for addition.

$$7 + 7 + 7 + 7 + 7 + 7 = 42$$
and
$$7 \times 6 = 42$$

Counting by 1s, 2s, 5s, and 10s was learned in 1st grade and reviewed in 2nd. Multiplication by 3s, 4s, 6s, 7s, 8s, and 9s should be mastered in the first half of the 3rd grade in order to lay the foundation for division in the second half.

Reviewing and learning multiplication and division facts up to **10 x 10** and **100 ÷ 10** can take up through the end of 3rd grade to memorize. Children also start to learn multiplication and division of two- and three-digit numbers by a single-digit number.

$$\begin{array}{ccc} 39 & 135 & \\ \underline{\times 3} & \underline{\times 6} & 7\,\overline{)28}^{\,4} \end{array}$$

A good check for children just learning to multiply is to remember that when both numbers multiplied are even, the answer will be even. When one number is even and the other odd, the answer will still be even. The answer is only odd when both numbers multiplied are odd.

Once a child has arrived at an answer (any of the four operations), it can be easily checked by the reverse operation. For example, when multiplying **8 x 4 = 32**, the answer can be checked by doing the problem in reverse—division: **32 ÷ 4 = 8**.

Third grade probabilities are encountered in tally exercises where children predict the probability of an event, such as heads and tails in a coin toss. The coins are then tossed and the actual results are noted.

Statistics are used when reading simple graphs in order to obtain the data and convert it to usable information. In order to convert data from chart form to sentence form, children need to practice gathering information and creating their own charts first. This way, they are familiar with the types of underlying facts that go into a chart. Spatial visualization is necessary to understand graphs (correlating two sets of information) and fractions (parts of a whole).

Common difficulties

1. **Multi-step problems**
   With double-digit multiplication, long division, and longer series of sums, children need to hold more information in their heads for a longer period of time while doing these multi-step computations. There are two things that support a child's memory. One is a good command of the basic arithmetic facts, because that lessens the time needed to finish the problem. The other is a good understanding of the whole problem, which has to do with place holders and columns for carrying and borrowing.

2. **Complex word problems**
   When children first learned word problems, there was generally one operation that needed to be completed. In the 3rd grade, there are frequently many steps and a variety of functions. For example, the following typical problem contains two functions, division and addition:

   A sailboat traveling 50 miles per hour took a 250 mile trip. If the sailors left at 9 a.m., what time did they return?

   First you have to divide (**250 ÷ 50**) to find out how long the trip took. Then you have to add the hours to 9 a.m. for the answer of 2 p.m.

More 3rd grade skills

♦ **Times tables**

In the 3rd grade, children are expected to know the times table up to 10 x 10. Work with your child until each set of numbers is mastered.

1	2	3	4	5	6	7	8	9	10
2	4	6	8	10	12	14	16	18	20
3	6	9	12	15	18	21	24	27	30
4	8	12	16	20	24	28	32	36	40
5	10	15	20	25	30	35	40	45	50
6	12	18	24	30	36	42	48	54	60
7	14	21	28	35	42	49	56	63	70
8	16	24	32	40	48	56	64	72	80
9	18	27	36	45	54	63	72	81	90
10	20	30	40	50	60	70	80	90	100

♦ **Times tables—9s**

Nines are magical, of course. One of the easiest tricks you can do with 9s is a quick multiplication technique.

When 9 is multiplied by a number (3, for example), the number in the tens column of the answer (27) will be one less than the number you are multiplying by (**9 x 3 = 27**) and the two numbers of the answer will always add up to 9 (**2 + 7 = 9**)!

Here's a chart to
illustrate this
technique:

0	**9**
1	**8**
2	**7**
3	**6**
4	**5**
5	**4**
6	**3**
7	**2**
8	**1**
9	**0**

♦ **Squares**

Squares are important in the practical world
in terms of measuring floor space or other
shapes. They also lead into roots and powers,
which can be written in exponential notation.
(2 x 2 = 4 or 2²)

5^2

1	2	3	4	5	6	7	8	9	10
2	4	6	8	10	12	14	16	18	20
3	6	9	12	15	18	21	24	27	30
4	8	12	16	20	24	28	32	36	40
5	10	15	20	25	30	35	40	45	50
6	12	18	24	30	36	42	48	54	60
7	14	21	28	35	42	49	56	63	70
8	16	24	32	40	48	56	64	72	80
9	18	27	36	45	54	63	72	81	90
10	20	30	40	50	60	70	80	90	100

♦ **Decimals**

In the 3rd grade, children should become
familiar with the concept of decimals and
percentages. An easy way for a 3rd grader to
grasp this is in terms of 100 cents being equal
to *one whole* dollar. Then any amount less than

the whole, 67 cents, for example, can be .67 of a dollar (a whole) which is the same as 67%.

◆ Standard measurements
In the 3rd grade, measurements are also learned, generally consisting of *lengths, volume, weights,* and *temperature.*

Standard Ruler Facts	Abbreviations	
12 inches in a foot	inch	in.
36 inches in a yard	foot	ft.
3 feet in a yard	yard	yd.

Standard Volume Facts	Abbreviations	
8 ounces in a cup	ounce	oz.
2 cups in a pint	pint	pt.
2 pints in a quart	quart	qt.
4 quarts in a gallon	gallon	gal.

Fluid Weight

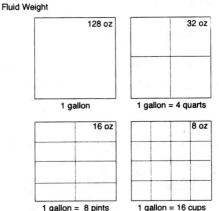

Standard Weight Facts	Abbreviations	
8 ounces in a cup	ounce	oz.
16 ounces in a pound	pound	lb.

Temperature Facts	Abbreviations
32°F is freezing	Fahrenheit F
212°F is boiling	degree deg.

◆ Metric measurements

Metric refers to *meter*, which is the basis for this system. It is based on divisions of 1, 10, 100, and 1,000. It is used exclusively in most countries outside the United States. In recent years, the metric system has come to be used in many aspects of American life.

Metric Ruler Facts	Abbreviations
10 millimeters in a centimeter	millimeter mm
100 centimeters in a meter	centimeter cm
1,000 millimeters in a meter	meter m
1,000 meters in a kilometer	kilometer km

Metric Volume Facts	Abbreviations
1,000 milliliters in a liter	milliliter ml
A liter is a little smaller than a quart	liter l

Metric Weight Facts	Abbreviations
1,000 milligrams in a gram	milligram mg
1,000 grams in a kilogram	gram g
A kilogram is 2.2 pounds	kilogram kg

Temperature Facts	Abbreviations
0°C is freezing	Centigrade C
100°C is boiling	degree deg.

◆ Short division

The first big step in the early part of 3rd grade was multiplication. The next big step toward the end of 3rd grade is the introduction of division. Just as addition and subtraction started off with no regrouping, so does division. This is called short division.

$$\begin{array}{r} \text{quotient} \ \ \textbf{5} \\ \text{divisor} \ \textbf{5} \overline{\smash{)}\ \textbf{25}} \ \text{dividend} \end{array} \qquad \textbf{25 ÷ 5 = 5}$$

These problems can be expressed as *25 divided by 5,* or *5 goes into 25.* Because 5 goes into 25 an even number of times, there is no remainder.

With division, a student can always check his work by multiplying the quotient (**5**) by the divisor (**5**). **5 x 5 = 25**, which is the original dividend.

◆ Simple fractions
The third big step in the 3rd grade is fractions. It's important to realize that fractions and division are the same thing.

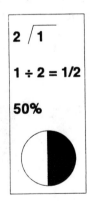

2 / 1

1 ÷ 2 = 1/2

50%

What are fractions?
Fractions are *parts* of a *whole.* The most simple and common fraction is **1/2**, which is **1 ÷ 2**, or one part out of a whole divided into two equal parts.

In terms of what has been presented so far, the connections have been addition and its opposite, subtraction; addition and its short form; and multiplication and its opposite, division. Now we come to division and its short form, fractions. In a nutshell, fractions are division. 4/5 is simply

$$5\overline{)4}$$

5 can't go into **4**, so a **0** preceded by a decimal point needs to be added after the **4**.

$$5\overline{)4.0}^{\,.8}$$

The answer is **.8**, which is the same as **80%**. So **4/5 = 80%**.

Another key fact to remember about fractions is that when the numerator is the same, the *larger the denominator*, the *smaller the fraction (the piece of the whole)*.

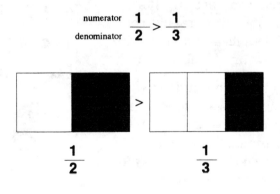

Fourth Grade

Basic skills

By the 4th grade, a student should be able to add, subtract, multiply, and divide single and multiple whole numbers with multiple steps, quickly and accurately, as well as add and subtract simple decimal numbers and percentages such as 10%, 50%, and 100%.

Basic geometry comes into play in the 4th grade, including such concepts as right, acute, and obtuse angles.

Children in 4th grade should also be able to estimate measurements, and use standard units to measure length, area, weight, volume, and temperature.

Both digital and analog clocks should be used to tell time for purposes such as calculating a duration or determining a time in the past or future, including crossing the meridian from a.m. to p.m.

Probability and statistics at this level include sampling techniques in order to collect information or to conduct a survey, then collating the data into a graph (*pie, bar,* or *line*), and averaging the results.

Common difficulties

---

1. **Alignment in division**
   One of the most difficult skills at this level is lining up long division problems. Children don't always realize why they are moving over—they just memorize the process of indenting and bringing down the next number in the dividend. The key to understanding is in place holders, which show that we are moving from ones to

tens to hundreds and so on. Either writing in the zeros or using grid paper makes short work of long division. Look at the difference in these two examples:

```
          192696                  192696
      5 / 963480             5 / 963480
        −5                       500000
        ───                      ──────
        46                       460000
       −45                       450000
       ───                       ──────
        13                        13000
       −10                        10000
       ───                        ──────
        34                         3400
       −30                         3000
       ───                         ──────
        48                          480
       −45                          450
       ───                          ───
        30                           30
       −30                           30
       ───                          ───
         0                            0
```

2. **Mechanics of long division**
   It's easy to lose track in long division, so it's helpful to remember that it's a pattern:

   division → multiplication → subtraction;
   division → multiplication → subtraction,

   over and over until the end.

3. **Place holders and commas**
   Children often forget to put the commas in numbers larger than 100. The rule is one comma for every three digits, starting from the ones place:

   1,000; 10,000; 100,000; 1,000,000.

4. **Aligning the decimal point**
   The decimal point marks the boundary

between a whole number and the decimal fraction. The point always lines up, no matter how many numbers there are. For example:

$$\begin{array}{r} 3.75 \\ +\ \underline{0.50} \\ 4.25 \end{array} \qquad \begin{array}{r} 3.000 \\ +\ \underline{0.003} \\ 3.003 \end{array}$$

5. **Understanding the concept of fractions**
   Children should be able to understand that fractions are parts of a whole and that the same amount—half, for example—can be written in many ways. At first, it is difficult to grasp what fractions and their equivalencies are, that **1/2** and **2/4** are the same as **4/8** and **5/10** of a whole, and that **.5 = 50/100 = 5/10 = 1/2**. Explain fractions to your child by using tangible examples, such as pieces of a pie.

6. **Converting charts to words**
   Charts are visual representations of numbers (amounts, duration, etc.), and children must be able to change what they see in a chart into clear sentences and accurate computations.

More 4th grade skills

♦ **Long division**
   When the dividend cannot be evenly divided by the divisor, there will be an amount left over. If the amount is smaller than the divisor, it will be a remainder.

```
      5 R 1
5 / 26
```

If the amount is larger, it will be divided by the divisor and the problem becomes long division. Depending on the dividend, there may still be a remainder.

```
     33                    33 R 1
5 / 165              5 / 166
  −150                  −150
    15                    16
  −15                    −15
     0                     1
```

Here are the steps:

1. The divisor, **5**, can't go into the first number of the dividend, **1**.

2. Calculate how many times the divisor **5** goes into **16** (<u>three</u> times), with **1** left over.

3. Write the **3** above the line, directly over the **6**.

4. Write the **15** below the **16** and add a place holder **0**.

5. Subtract **150** from **165**.

6. Write the difference, **15**.

7. Calculate how many times the divisor **5** will go into **15** (<u>three</u> times).

8. Write **3** above the line, to the right of the other **3**. This gives the answer **33**.

♦ Double digit multiplication

When a child gets to the double digits, you should get out the graph paper. There is a lot of aligning, and one misalignment will result in an incorrect answer. As with the other functions, it is important to align the numbers in the correct columns—ones, tens and so on.

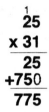

$$\begin{array}{r} \overset{1}{2}5 \\ \times\,31 \\ \hline 25 \\ +750 \\ \hline 775 \end{array}$$

1. Multiply **1** times **5**. Write <u>**5**</u> below the **1**.

2. Multiply **1** times **2**. Write <u>**2**</u> below the **3**.

3. Add a place holder **0** below the **5**.

4. Multiply **3** times **5**. Write <u>**5**</u> below the **2**.

5. Carry the **1** (over the **2** in **25**).

6. Multiply **3** times **2**. Add the carried **1**.

7. Write <u>**7**</u> to the left of the **5**.

8. Add **25** and **750**.

9. The total is **775**.

♦ Multiple digit division

Multiple digit division is not much different from single digit division.

```
            91 R 12
     14 / 1286
         −1260
           26
          −14
           12
```

1. Estimate the result to compare against the final total. This will eliminate large errors. **14 x 10** is **140**, so **10** is too high. Try **14 x 9**. **126** does go into **128**. This tells you that your answer will be approximately **90**.

2. **14** goes into **128 9** times (with **2** left over).

3. Write the **9** above the line, directly over the **8**.

4. Multiply **9** by **14**. **9 x 14 = 126**.

5. Write the **126** below the **128** and add a place holder **0**.

6. Subtract **1,260** from **1,286**.

7. Write the difference, **26**.

8. **14** goes into **26 1** time (with **12** left over).

9. Write the **1** over the **6**.

10. Multiply the **1** by **14**. **1 x 14 = 14**.

11. Subtract **14** from **26**. **26 - 14 = 12**.

12. **14** does not go into **12**. So **12** is the remainder.

13. The answer is **91** remainder **12**. The answer can also be written **91 12/14**, which reduces to **91 6/7**.

♦ Rounding and estimating

Accuracy is very important in arithmetic, but not always necessary. Two skills to be mastered in the 4th grade are *estimating* and *rounding off.*

Estimating is making an educated guess. For example, if you need to find out how large a room is, but you don't need the exact inches, you can estimate by "pacing off" to find the general number.

Rounding off is a way of removing the insignificant digits from the equation so that you can work with the significant digits. For example, if you are talking about $1,000, it doesn't matter about a few dollars one way or the other. Tens of dollars may not be highly significant either. The first decision is what digit is significant for your estimation—and that will probably be 100s, and definitely 1,000s. So if something costs $985 dollars, that number can be rounded up to the next 100, which brings it to $1,000.

However, rounding off needs to be balanced in order not to skew high or low. If you always round up, then the total will be high and always rounding down will pull down the total.

In order to counter this skewing, round up half the time and round down the other half. Here are some general rules to follow:

Number ends in	Process
0	Leave it as it is
1, 2, 3, 4	Round down
6, 7, 8, 9	Round up
5	Look at the preceding number; if it is odd (3̲5), round up; if it is even (4̲5), round down. If there is no preceding number, round down.

♦ **Geometry**

Fourth grade geometry is limited to lines and angles. Children need to know the two main line relationships. They also need to know the three basic angles and the rules for them.

Lines

Angles

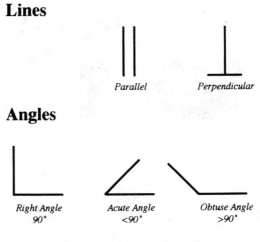

Parallel   Perpendicular

Right Angle *90°*   Acute Angle *<90°*   Obtuse Angle *>90°*

♦ **Comparing fractions**
In the 3rd grade, it was introduced that with
fractions, when the numerator is the same,
the *larger the denominator*, the *smaller the
fraction*. This is the case when comparing
unlike fractions. (An unlike fraction is
when the denominators are different.)

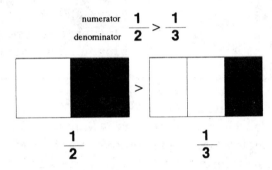

When comparing like fractions, the *larger the
numerator*, the *greater the amount*.

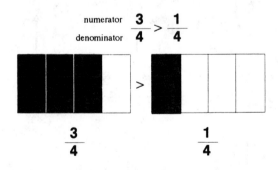

♦ **Tables and graphs**
A 4th grader should be able to read and
interpret graphs (stable, erratic, increasing,
decreasing, etc.) and make a line graph for

each set of data, with a title and labeling for the vertical scale and the horizontal scale. The first step is to find the *range of the data,* choose an interval that best represents it, and mark off equal spaces on the vertical scale. Then round off the data to the nearest 10. The scale should begin with zero. The vertical scale notes time (years, in this case).

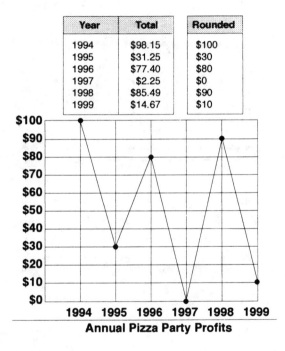

Year	Total	Rounded
1994	$98.15	$100
1995	$31.25	$30
1996	$77.40	$80
1997	$2.25	$0
1998	$85.49	$90
1999	$14.67	$10

Annual Pizza Party Profits

◆ **Averaging**
Averaging is a simple yet useful math skill. It is particularly convenient with graphs. Once a chart has been plotted, it's helpful to eliminate the highs and the lows and find out what the middle is.

Averaging is adding and dividing. In the previous graph, there were six dollar amounts. The rounded numbers totaled **$310**. Divide **$310** by **6** and the average amount for 1994–1999 was **$52**.

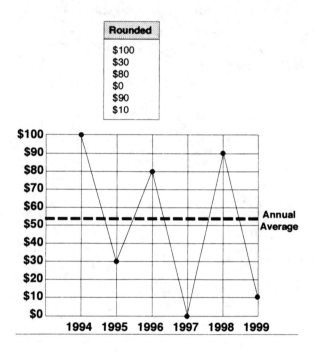

Rounded
$100
$30
$80
$0
$90
$10

Fifth Grade

Basic skills

In the 5th grade, children review, consolidate, and build upon the principles acquired in the previous years.

They hone their skills in the four functions (addition, subtraction, multiplication, and division) with whole numbers, as well as with fractions, decimals, numeral problems, word problems, and graphs. They learn how to compute percentages and relate percentages to fractions and decimals. They need to understand fraction relationships: *comparisons* (3/5 > 1/2), *equivalence* (2/3 = 4/6), *reducing* (3/9 = 1/3), and *mixed numbers* (1 1/3) vs. *improper fractions* (4/3).

By this time, because they have mastered the basics, they can go on to using a calculator for computation as they work alone or in cooperative groups. Concentration, comprehension, and focus should be at the point where the child does not lose track in a multiple-step problem.

Commonalties are used in the 5th grade, with *common divisors* and *common multiples*.

Fifth grade geometry deals with *circle* relationships, including *diameter, circumference,* and *radius,* along with recognizing, measuring, and drawing angles of various kinds.

Fifth graders should have no trouble converting or reducing fractions and are in a position to compute fractions with the four functions.

Arithmetic is intuitive—if you divide a number, it gets smaller. When you divide by a fraction, the number gets bigger, because rather than dividing something into parts, you are counting parts of a whole. For example, if you are dividing the number **4** into **1/10**, you are dividing 4 *wholes* into 10 parts each. So you end up with 40 parts.

Division of a Fraction

4 ÷ 1/10 = 40

Common difficulties

1. **Borrowing in subtracting fractions**
   When the problem involves regrouping, it is a difficult concept to think of breaking up the whole number and carrying it over to the fraction *as a fraction*. If you have the problem

   2 ¼ – 1 ¾ =

   you have to convert the numbers to fractions with a common denominator (which they already have in this case). This is done as follows: For each mixed number (**2 1/4**, for example), multiply the whole number (**2**) by the denominator (**4** or a *fourth*). This will tell you how many *fourths* are in the whole number **2** (8). To that add the fourth you already had (**1/4**). You now have **9/4**. Hence, **2 1/4** is equal to **9/4**.

   4 x 2 + 1 = 9 → 9/4

   4 x 1 + 3 = 7 → 7/4

   Then subtract.

   9/4 – 7/4 = 2/4 (or 1/2)

2. **Decimal place values**
    Remember that the number *left* of the decimal is the whole number, and the number *right* of the decimal is the fraction.

    ### 3.4 = 3 4/10

    .4 and **.40** are the same because in both the **4** is in the tenths place. However, **.04** would be **4/100**, because the **4** is in the hundredths place, hence **.04** is 4 hundredths.

3. **Converting mixed fractions**
    Converting an improper fraction such as **7/5** to a mixed fraction is simple division. An easy way to convert it is by dividing the numerator by the denominator (**7 ÷ 5**) and then writing the remainder as a fraction with the whole number equaling **1** (**1 2/5**). The remainder is the numerator and the denominator stays the same.

4. **Crossing from a.m. to p.m.**
    The problem with clocks is that most things are on a base 10 system, but time is base 12. This makes it difficult to go from 8 p.m. to 2 a.m., as the meridian must be crossed. Have your child count from 8 to 12 (4 hours) and then from 12 to 2 (2 hours), and add them together (6 hours).

5. **Common factors**
    A factor is one of two or more quantities that divides a given quantity without a remainder. For example, 2 has two factors, **2** and **1**. The number 6 has four factors, **1**, **6**, **2**, and **3**

because all can be divided into 6 without a remainder.

$$6 \div 6 = 1$$
$$6 \div 1 = 6$$
$$6 \div 3 = 2$$
$$6 \div 2 = 3$$

Factors are used in reducing fractions and finding common denominators.

More 5th grade skills

♦ **Geometry**
Fifth grade geometry expands upon angles and includes circles. Children should understand circle relationships, including the diameter, circumference, and radius. They should be able to recognize congruent shapes (the same size or shape) when they are in different positions.

Circles

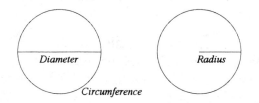

Diameter

Circumference

Radius

Congruent shapes

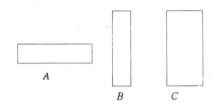

A and B are congruent shapes because they both measure ¼ by 1. B and C are not congruent (although they are both rectangles) because C is wider.

◆ **Adding and subtracting fractions**
When you are adding or subtracting **like fractions** (common denominator), you just add or subtract the numerators, and the denominator stays the same.

$$\frac{1}{4} + \frac{1}{4} = \boxed{\frac{2}{4}} = \boxed{\frac{1}{2}}$$

When you are adding or subtracting **unlike fractions**, you need to find a common denominator before completing the computation.

The least common denominator (LCD) of unlike fractions (**1/4** and **1/6**, for example) is the lowest number that is a multiple of each of the denominators:

The multiples of 4: **4**, **8**, **12**, **16**, **20**, **24** ...

The multiples of 6: **6**, **12**, **18**, **24**, **30**, **36** ...

The least common multiple is **12**. Use the LCD to write like fractions for **1/4** and **1/6**.

---

1. Calculate how many times each of the uncommon denominators (**4** and **6**) can go into the common denominator (**12**). **4** goes into **12, 3** times. **6** goes into **12, 2** times.

2. Multiply the **1/4** by **3/3** and the **1/6** by **2/2.**

$$\frac{1}{4} \times \frac{3}{3} = \frac{3}{12}$$

$$\frac{1}{6} \times \frac{2}{2} = \frac{2}{12}$$

3. Now you have like fractions to work with.

$$\frac{3}{12} + \frac{2}{12} = \frac{5}{12}$$

♦ **Reducing fractions**
When reducing a fraction, the first thing is to see if the denominator can be divided by the numerator, as in the following example:

$$\frac{6}{12} \div \frac{6}{6} = \frac{1}{2}$$

If the denominator can't be divided by the numerator, try to find a number that goes into both the top and the bottom numbers. For example:

$$\frac{9}{12} \div \frac{3}{3} = \frac{3}{4}$$

In a word problem or in a practical situation, the fraction or remainder must be treated as a whole. If you have a car that holds 4 people, and 10 people are going somewhere, you want to find out how many cars you need. If you do the math, it will come out to be 2 1/2 cars. In real life, of course, this is impractical, so you need 3 cars.

♦ **Multiplying and dividing fractions**
With whole numbers, addition and subtraction is easier than multiplication and division. With fractions, however, multiplication and division are actually easier than addition and subtraction, because you don't have to find a common denominator.

Multiplication: Simply multiply the numerator by the numerator and the denominator by the denominator.

$$\frac{3}{4} \times \frac{2}{3} = \boxed{\frac{6}{12}}$$

To reduce this answer, divide the numerator and the denominator by **6**.

$$\boxed{\frac{6}{12}} \div \frac{6}{6} = \boxed{\frac{1}{3}}$$

Division: The first fraction stays as it is and the second (the divisor) gets inverted. So,

$$\frac{3}{4} \div \frac{2}{3} = \boxed{}$$

becomes:

$$\frac{3}{4} \times \frac{3}{2} = \frac{9}{8} = \boxed{1\frac{1}{8}}$$

♦ **Converting fractions to decimals**
Because fractions and decimals are the same thing (division), this is an extremely simple process. Simply divide the numerator by the denominator.

$$\boxed{\frac{1}{2}} = 2\overline{)1} = 2\overline{)1.0}^{.5} = \boxed{.5}$$

♦ **Converting decimals to fractions**
This is even easier, because the decimal point tells you that it's a fraction.

$$\boxed{.5} = \frac{5}{10} = \boxed{\frac{1}{2}}$$

The number to the right of the point is the numerator. The denominator is always 1 followed by as many 0s as there are number places after the point. For example:

.1 = 1/10   .01 = 1/100   .001 = 1/1000

.5 = 5/10   .15 = 15/100 .625 = 625/1000

Again, this is easily understood by knowing place values. Whereas in whole numbers we work with ones, tens, hundreds, and so on, in decimals, we work with—from left to right— tenths, hundredths, thousandths, and so on. Percentage is just *per 100*. **15% = 15/100**.

The decimal equivalents of these common fractions should be memorized:

Aliquot Parts		
1.00	=	1
.50	=	1/2
.25	=	1/4
.125	=	1/8
.0625	=	1/16

Reciprocals				
1	x	1.00	=	1
2	x	.50	=	1
4	x	.25	=	1
8	x	.125	=	1
16	x	.0625	=	1

◆ **Graphs and tables**
Fifth graders are in the position to present information in a variety of forms. In a survey, for example, a student will first collect the basic information. This can be presented in paragraph form.

> *Raw data: There are 25 students, 12 boys and 13 girls. They are majoring in math, English, history, biology, and PE.*

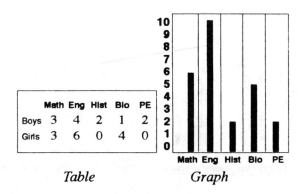

	Math	Eng	Hist	Bio	PE
Boys	3	4	2	1	2
Girls	3	6	0	4	0

Table   *Graph*

Numbers can be presented in a table, which is an arrangement of data in columns and rows.

Comparisons can be presented in a graph, which is a picture to illustrate quantitative relationships.

Fifth graders should be able to gather the data, compile it into a table, and present the findings in a graph. They should also be able to read a table or a graph and extrapolate the basic information.

Students should be able to select what they feel is the pertinent comparison and present it in graph form, with a corresponding legend to explain what is being compared within a category.

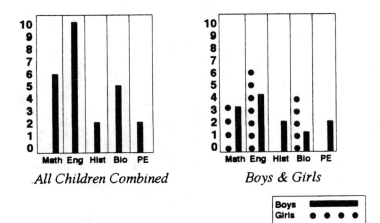

All Children Combined   *Boys & Girls*

| Boys | ▬▬▬ |
| Girls | ● ● ● ● |

A 5th grader should be confident and accurate converting data among the three main graph formats: *bar, line,* and *pie.*

Types of Graphs or Charts

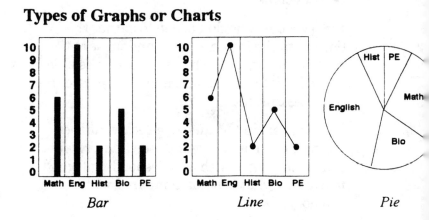

Bar   *Line*   *Pie*

Reassessments

Kindergarten
through
Fifth Grade

Shapes & Sizes

Kindergarten

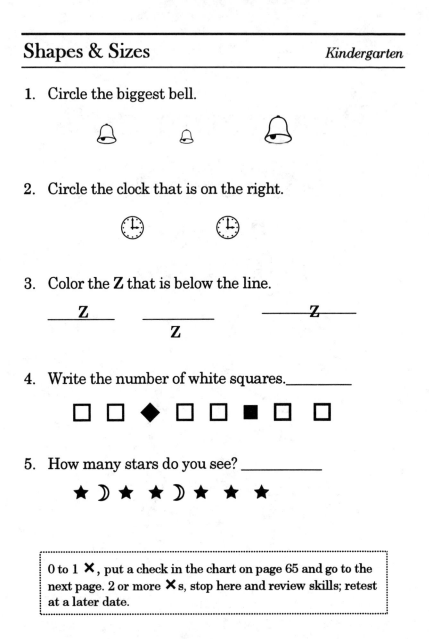

1. Circle the biggest bell.

2. Circle the clock that is on the right.

3. Color the **Z** that is below the line.

4. Write the number of white squares._____

5. How many stars do you see? _____

0 to 1 ✖, put a check in the chart on page 65 and go to the next page. 2 or more ✖s, stop here and review skills; retest at a later date.

Patterns & Counting

Kindergarten

1. Draw a line from the number to the group that it matches.

    1
    2
    3
    4
    5

2. How many baloons do you see? _____

3. Color the circle blue, the square yellow, and the triangle red.

4. Color the matching shape.

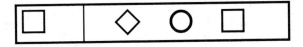

5. Circle the group that has the most in it.

0 to 1 ✗, put a check in the chart on page 65 and go to the next page. 2 or more ✗ s, stop here and review skills; retest at a later date.

Recognizing Numbers 1-10 *Kindergarten*

Have your child say each number.

	✓	✗	answer given
6	☐	☐	_____
7	☐	☐	_____
0	☐	☐	_____
4	☐	☐	_____
8	☐	☐	_____
5	☐	☐	_____
3	☐	☐	_____
1	☐	☐	_____
9	☐	☐	_____
2	☐	☐	_____

> ✓ = immediate response ✗ = slow or incorrect response
> 0 to 2 ✗ s, put a check in the chart on page 65 and go to the next page. 3 or more ✗ s, stop here and review skills; retest at a later date.

Writing Numbers 1-10 *Kindergarten*

Have your child write each number on his own, in order.
Start with 0 and work up to 10.

_____

_____

_____

_____

_____

_____

_____

_____

_____

_____

_____

0 to 2 **✗** s, put a check in the chart on page 65 and go to the
next page. 3 or more **✗** s, stop here and review skills; retest
at a later date.

Recognizing Numbers 1-100 *First Grade*

Have your child say each number.

	✓	✗	answer given
18	☐	☐	_____
31	☐	☐	_____
75	☐	☐	_____
28	☐	☐	_____
88	☐	☐	_____
63	☐	☐	_____
42	☐	☐	_____
94	☐	☐	_____
58	☐	☐	_____
89	☐	☐	_____

✓ = immediate response ✗ = slow or incorrect response
0 to 2 ✗s, put a check in the chart on page 65 and go to the next page. 3 or more ✗s, stop here and review skills; retest at a later date.

Writing Numbers 1-100 *First Grade*

Dictate the following numbers to your child and have him write them on the line.

fifty seven _____

twenty six _____

nineteen _____

seventy nine _____

thirty four _____

forty five _____

sixty two _____

eighty _____

one hundred and four _____

ninety three _____

---

0 to 2 ✖ s, put a check in the chart on page 65 and go to the next page. 3 or more ✖ s, stop here and review skills; retest at a later date.

Signs & Skip Counting

First Grade

Fill in the blanks by counting by 2s.

    1.   4   6   _____   10   12

    2.   8 _____ _____ _____ 16

Fill in the blanks by counting by 3s.

    3.   5 _____   11   14 _____

    4.   1 _____ _____   10 _____

Put the correct sign on the line (>, <, =).

    5.   4 _____   7

    6.   2 _____   0

    7.   19 _____   18

    8.   2 _____   1+1

    9.   13 _____   17

    10. 50 _____   50

0 to 2 ✖s, put a check in the chart on page 65 and go to the next page. 3 or more ✖s, stop here and review skills; retest at a later date.

Sequencing & Ordering   *First Grade*

Answer the following questions.

1. What is one more than 29? _____
2. What is one less than 50?_____
3. What is ten more than 44? _____
4. What is ten less than 62? _____
5. What is five less than 25? _____

Fill in the missing numbers.

6. 5   10   15   _____   _____
7. 22   24   26   _____   _____
8. 400   500   600   _____   _____
9. 197   198   199   _____   _____

Circle the larger number in each set.

10. 7   2   12. 2   18
11. 5   13   13. 24   42

Rewrite each set from the smallest to the largest.

14.   8   15   12   6   2

_____   _____   _____   _____   _____

15.   115   136   3   25   16

_____   _____   _____   _____   _____

0 to 3 ✘ s, put a check in the chart on page 65 and go to the next page. 4 or more ✘ s, stop here and review skills; retest at a later date.

Single & Double Digit Addition   *First Grade*

Solve the following problems.

1. $\begin{array}{r} 7 \\ + 3 \\ \hline \end{array}$ 6. $\begin{array}{r} 81 \\ + 15 \\ \hline \end{array}$

2. $\begin{array}{r} 8 \\ + 5 \\ \hline \end{array}$ 7. $\begin{array}{r} 53 \\ + 37 \\ \hline \end{array}$

3. $\begin{array}{r} 2 \\ + 6 \\ \hline \end{array}$ 8. $\begin{array}{r} 48 \\ + 35 \\ \hline \end{array}$

4. $\begin{array}{r} 4 \\ + 5 \\ \hline \end{array}$ 9. $\begin{array}{r} 19 \\ + 67 \\ \hline \end{array}$

5. $\begin{array}{r} 5 \\ + 3 \\ \hline \end{array}$ 10. $\begin{array}{r} 35 \\ + 61 \\ \hline \end{array}$

0 to 2 ✖s, put a check in the chart on page 65 and go to the next page. 3 or more ✖s, stop here and review skills; retest at a later date.

Single & Double Digit Subtraction   *First Grade*

Solve the following problems.

1.
$$\begin{array}{r} 8 \\ -\,5 \\ \hline \end{array}$$

6.
$$\begin{array}{r} 64 \\ -\,11 \\ \hline \end{array}$$

2.
$$\begin{array}{r} 5 \\ -\,4 \\ \hline \end{array}$$

7.
$$\begin{array}{r} 49 \\ -\,38 \\ \hline \end{array}$$

3.
$$\begin{array}{r} 54 \\ -\,14 \\ \hline \end{array}$$

8.
$$\begin{array}{r} 46 \\ -\,22 \\ \hline \end{array}$$

4.
$$\begin{array}{r} 7 \\ -\,3 \\ \hline \end{array}$$

9.
$$\begin{array}{r} 87 \\ -\,44 \\ \hline \end{array}$$

5.
$$\begin{array}{r} 6 \\ -\,3 \\ \hline \end{array}$$

10.
$$\begin{array}{r} 68 \\ -\,25 \\ \hline \end{array}$$

0 to 2 ✘s, put a check in the chart on page 65 and go to the next page. 3 or more ✘s, stop here and review skills; retest at a later date.

Time & Money

First Grade

Answer the following questions.

1. What time is it? _____

2. Draw hands on the
   clock to show 9:00.

3. About how long would it take to brush your teeth?

   ❑ 2 minutes   ❑ 2 hours

4. About how long is lunch recess at school?

   ❑ 1 minute   ❑ 1 hour

5. How much is each coin? Write the amount below
   the coin.

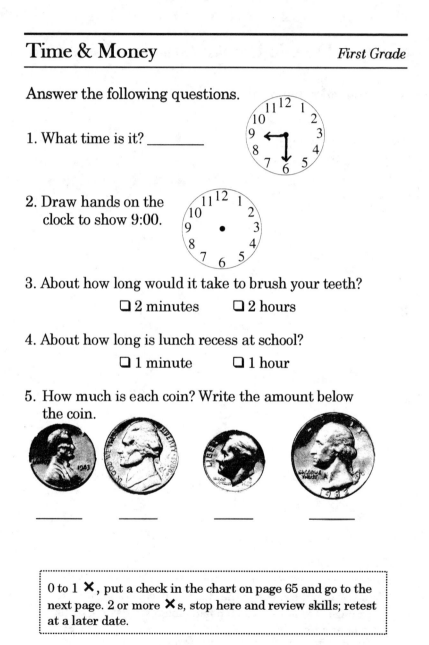

_____   _____   _____   _____

---

0 to 1 ✗, put a check in the chart on page 65 and go to the
next page. 2 or more ✗s, stop here and review skills; retest
at a later date.

Patterns

Copy the pattern.

1. ◇ △ □ ◇ _____

2. O ✗ O ✗ _____

What would come next?

3. ◇ □ ◇ □ ◇ □ _____

4. △ △ ▽ △ △ ▽ _____

5. **A 1 B 2 C 3 D** _____

0 to 1 ✗, put a check in the chart on page 65 and go to the next page. 2 or more ✗ s, stop here and review skills; retest at a later date.

Time & Money

Second Grade

1. What time is it? _____

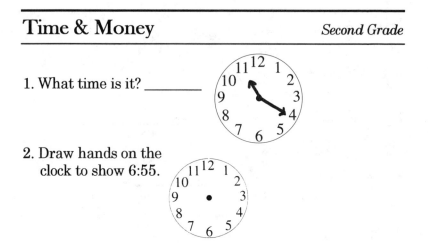

2. Draw hands on the clock to show 6:55.

3. Circle the set that is more.

4. How many quarters do you need to make one dollar?
   ❑ 10   ❑ 20   ❑ 4   ❑ 100

5. What is the total? _____

> 0 to 1 ✗, put a check in the chart on page 65 and go to the next page. 2 or more ✗ s, stop here and review skills; retest at a later date.

Computation with Regrouping   *Second Grade*

Solve the following problems.

1.   57
       + 24

6.   44
       − 25

2.   72
       + 57

7.   71
       − 44

3.   35
       + 65

8.   26
       − 18

4.   25
       + 56

9.   88
       − 79

5.   99
       + 11

10.   65
       − 48

0 to 2 ✗s, put a check in the chart on page 65 and go to the next page. 3 or more ✗s, stop here and review skills; retest at a later date.

Simple Fractions

Second Grade

Look at each picture and write the fraction, with the numerator represented by the white space, and the denominator by the dark space. A sample is given.

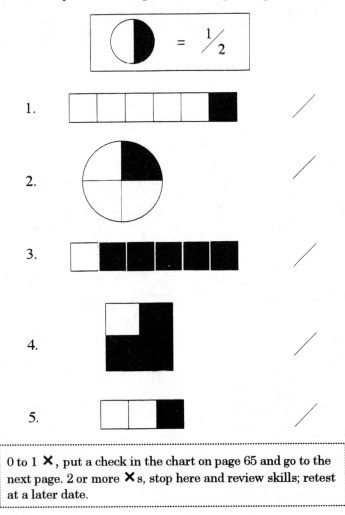

3 Digit Mixed Computation

Solve the following problems.

1.	358 + 645		6.	448 − 219
2.	845 − 517		7.	203 + 707
3.	842 + 178		8.	500 − 219
4.	555 + 555		9.	901 − 299
5.	816 − 807		10.	344 + 499

0 to 2 ✖s, put a check in the chart on page 65 and go to the next page. 3 or more ✖s, stop here and review skills; retest at a later date.

Word Problems

Second Grade

Read the following questions and mark the correct answer.

1. If a snail crawls 15 inches to the left and then 20 inches down, how many inches has it gone in all?

   _____

2. If there are 19 birds on a wire, and 11 fly away, how many birds are left?

   _____

3. 20 kids go out to recess on the playground. 5 kids go to the soccer field. 6 kids go to the monkey bars to play. The rest are in the sandbox. How many kids are in the sandbox?

   _____

4. Write the following words in number form: nine hundred fifty two

   _____

5. Write the following words in number form: three hundred eighty

   _____

0 to 1 ✖, put a check in the chart on page 65 and go to the next page. 2 or more ✖s, stop here and review skills; retest at a later date.

Single Digit Multiplication/Division *Third Grade*

Solve the following problems.

1. $\begin{array}{r} 8 \\ \times\,2 \\ \hline \end{array}$

6. $4 \times 4 =$

2. $2\,\overline{)\,6\,}$

7. $10 \div 2 =$

3. $\begin{array}{r} 3 \\ \times\,7 \\ \hline \end{array}$

8. $9 \times 5 =$

9. $10 \div 5 =$

4. $4\,\overline{)\,8\,}$

5. $\begin{array}{r} 7 \\ \times\,8 \\ \hline \end{array}$

10. $6 \times 8 =$

0 to 2 ✖s, put a check in the chart on page 65 and go to the next page. 3 or more ✖s, stop here and review skills; retest at a later date.

Double Digit Multiplication/Division *Third Grade*

Solve the following problems.

1. 23
x 3

6. 3 ⟌ 36

2. 8 ⟌ 24

7. 9 ⟌ 72

3. 36
x 3

8. 54
x 4

4. 6 ⟌ 24

9. 7 ⟌ 56

5. 56
x 7

10. 79
x 8

0 to 2 ✖s, put a check in the chart on page 65 and go to the next page. 3 or more ✖s, stop here and review skills; retest at a later date.

Time & Money   *Third Grade*

Solve the following word problems.

1. If it is 9:55 a.m. now, what time will it be in five hours?

    _____

2. Carla went to sleep at 8:30 p.m. and woke up at 6:30 a.m. How long did she sleep?

    _____

3. If a pair of shoes costs $22.75 and a shirt costs $24.25, how much do they cost together?

    _____

4. Tina has two dollars. She buys some candy that costs $1.59. How much change does she get?

    _____

5. Sam earns $15.50 per day. If he works for four days, how much does he earn?

    _____

0 to 1 ✗ , put a check in the chart on page 65 and go to the next page. 2 or more ✗ s, stop here and review skills; retest at a later date.

Graphs   *Third Grade*

Based on the graph, answer the following questions.

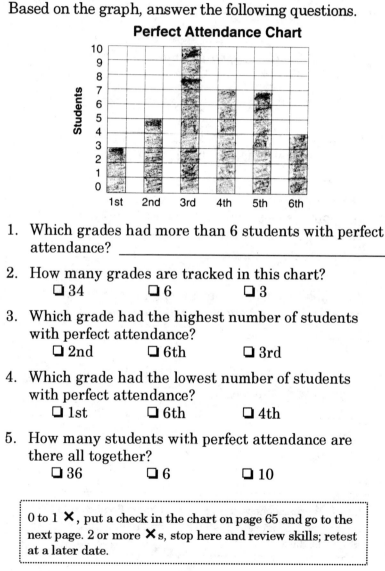

Perfect Attendance Chart

1. Which grades had more than 6 students with perfect attendance? _____

2. How many grades are tracked in this chart?
   ❏ 34   ❏ 6   ❏ 3

3. Which grade had the highest number of students with perfect attendance?
   ❏ 2nd   ❏ 6th   ❏ 3rd

4. Which grade had the lowest number of students with perfect attendance?
   ❏ 1st   ❏ 6th   ❏ 4th

5. How many students with perfect attendance are there all together?
   ❏ 36   ❏ 6   ❏ 10

---

0 to 1 ✖, put a check in the chart on page 65 and go to the next page. 2 or more ✖s, stop here and review skills; retest at a later date.

Division & Remainders

Solve the following division problems.

1. $5\overline{)6}$

6. $3\overline{)23}$

2. $4\overline{)41}$

7. $8\overline{)31}$

3. $7\overline{)55}$

8. $6\overline{)71}$

4. $9\overline{)200}$

9. $2\overline{)55}$

5. $5\overline{)98}$

10. $9\overline{)17}$

---

0 to 2 ✘ s, put a check in the chart on page 65 and go to the
next page. 3 or more ✘ s, stop here and review skills; retest
at a later date.

Mixed Word Problems

Third Grade

Read the following questions and write the correct answer.

1. If there are 7 days in a week and 4 weeks in a month, how many days are in that month?

    _____

2. If there are 8 shelves and each shelf holds 20 books, how many books are there?

    _____

3. The computer was on for 2 hours per day. At the end of 16 days, how long had it been on?

    _____

4. The marathon bike race was 60 miles long. The children rode an even amount each day for 5 days. How many miles did they ride each day?

    _____

5. Write the following words in number form:
    Seven hundred twenty nine thousand four hundred sixty eight

    _____

0 to 1 ✖, put a check in the chart on page 65 and go to the next page. 2 or more ✖ s, stop here and review skills; retest at a later date.

Rounding Off & Estimating   *Fourth Grade*

Round off each number to the nearest 10:

   1. 7   _____   2. 32 _____

Round off each number to the nearest 100:

   3. 225   _____   4. 369 _____

Estimate

5. 13 feet is approximately how many yards?

   _____

6. 35 inches is approximately how many feet?

   _____

7. 70 days is approximately how many months?

   _____

Average

8. Ben is 6 feet tall. Tim is 4 feet tall. Fred is 5 feet tall. What is the average height?

   _____

9. The holiday schedule is as follows: 7 days in March, 9 days in May, 3 days in June, 1 in July. What is the average?

   _____

10. Edgar earns $7 per day, working 4 days a week. What does that average per day for a 7-day week?

   _____

> 0 to 2 ✖s, put a check in the chart on page 65 and go to the next page. 3 or more ✖s, stop here and review skills; retest at a later date.

Multiple Digit Computing   *Fourth Grade*

Solve the following problems.

1.   25
      x 53

2.   29
      x 48

3.   57
      x 49

4.   83
      x 91

5.   11
      x 11

6.   8 $\overline{)354}$

7.   55 $\overline{)855}$

8.   22 $\overline{)\$3.51}$

9.   87 $\overline{)\$3.17}$

10.   40 $\overline{)500}$

> 0 to 2 ✖ s, put a check in the chart on page 65 and go to the next page. 3 or more ✖ s, stop here and review skills; retest at a later date.

Computing with Fractions

Fourth Grade

Reduce each fraction to its lowest terms.

1. $\dfrac{6}{8}$
        2. $\dfrac{16}{24}$
        3. $\dfrac{80}{100}$

Compare using >, <, = .

4. $\dfrac{1}{2}$ $\dfrac{1}{4}$
      5. $\dfrac{8}{9}$ $\dfrac{3}{4}$
      6. $\dfrac{1}{12}$ $\dfrac{2}{24}$

Reduce and write a mixed number or a whole number.

7. $\dfrac{5}{3}$
            8. $\dfrac{16}{4}$

9. $\dfrac{8}{3}$
            10. $\dfrac{9}{6}$

Add or subtract these fractions and reduce to lowest terms.

11. $2/5 + 2/5 =$
        12. $7\ 3/8 + 4\ 5/8 =$

13. $5/9 - 3/9 =$
        14. $1\ 6/10 + 3\ 2/10 =$

---

0 to 3 ✘ s, put a check in the chart on page 65 and go to the next page. 4 or more ✘ s, stop here and review skills; retest at a later date.

Measurements   *Fourth Grade*

Read the following questions and mark the correct answer.

1. If there are 4 kids playing and they need drinks, about how much juice would be needed for them altogether?
    ❑ a pint   ❑ a quart   ❑ a gallon

2. To measure how much carpeting would be needed to carpet your classroom floor, which measurement would be best to use?
    ❑ inches   ❑ feet   ❑ miles

3. To measure the weight of a serving of ice cream, which unit of measurement should be used?
    ❑ ounces   ❑ pounds   ❑ quarts

4. To measure how tall you are, which unit of measurement should be used?
    ❑ mm   ❑ cm   ❑ m   ❑ km

5. Compare using > or <.
    33 feet _____ 3 yards

0 to 1 ✖, put a check in the chart on page 65 and go to the next page. 2 or more ✖s, stop here and review skills; retest at a later date.

Mixed Word Problems

Fourth Grade

Read the following questions and check the correct answer.

1. What is the chance of drawing a silver coin from a can that has one silver coin and four gold ones?

   ❏ even   ❏ 1 in 4   ❏ 1 in 5

2. There are 12 children at the playground. Each one is then joined by one friend. Most of the children are on the swings, but four are at the slide. What portion of the kids are at the slide?

   ❏ 1/4   ❏ 1/5   ❏ 1/6

3. 68 children are going on a class trip. Each bus they're taking holds 20 children. How many buses are needed?

   ❏ 3 buses   ❏ 5 buses   ❏ 4 buses

4. Jack spent a quarter of his allowance on baseball cards, an eighth on bubble gum, and the rest on a gift for his mom. How much of his allowance did he spend on his mom?

   ❏ 1/2   ❏ 5/8   ❏ 3/6

5. Half of the kids in class had on white shirts, a quarter had on yellow shirts, an eighth had on blue shirts, and the rest had on orange shirts. How many kids had on orange shirts?

   ❏ 1/4   ❏ 1/8   ❏ 1/2

---

0 to 1 ✖, put a check in the chart on page 65 and go to the next page. 2 or more ✖s, stop here and review skills; retest at a later date.

Multiplying & Dividing Fractions   *Fifth Grade*

Multiply or divide these fractions. Reduce if necessary.

1. 1/3   x   2/3   =

2. 3/4   x   1/5   =

3. 5/6   x   2/3   =

4. 1/8   x   1/8   =

5. 1/2   x   3/1   =

6. 1/2   ÷   2/3   =

7. 1/8   ÷   7/10   =

8. 3/4   ÷   1/2   =

9. 1/3   ÷   3/1   =

10. 1/5   ÷   1/5   =

0 to 2 ✖ s, put a check in the chart on page 65 and go to the next page. 3 or more ✖ s, stop here and review skills; retest at a later date.

Graphs

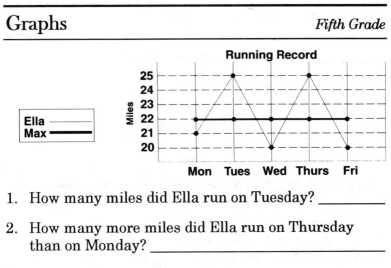

1. How many miles did Ella run on Tuesday? _____

2. How many more miles did Ella run on Thursday than on Monday? _____

3. Who ran further, Ella or Max? _____

4. What fraction of the time is spent at the beach?
   ❑ 1/8   ❑ 1/4   ❑ 1/2   ❑ 1   ❑ 2   ❑ 4

5. How much more time is spent at school than at the park?
   ❑ 1/8   ❑ 1/4   ❑ 1/2   ❑ 1   ❑ 2   ❑ 4

---

0 to 1 ✖, put a check in the chart on page 65 and go to the next page. 2 or more ✖ s, stop here and review skills; retest at a later date.

Tables

Fifth Grade

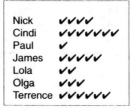

Summer Book-a-Thon

Nick	✔✔✔✔
Cindi	✔✔✔✔✔✔
Paul	✔
James	✔✔✔✔✔
Lola	✔✔
Olga	✔✔✔
Terrence	✔✔✔✔✔✔

1. How many books did the children read in all?

   _____

2. If Cindi received 25 cents for every book she read, how much money did she bring in?

   _____

3. What is the average number of books read?

   _____

	# of Days		# of Days
January	31	July	31
February	28	August	31
March	31	September	30
April	30	October	31
May	31	November	30
June	30	December	31

4. If today is January 2, how many more days until Valentines Day (February 14?) _____

5. What is the average number of days per month in the second half of the year? _____

---

0 to 1 ✖, put a check in the chart on page 65 and go to the next page. 2 or more ✖s, stop here and review skills; retest at a later date.

Measurements

Fifth Grade

1. Yesterday the temperature was 40° C. Was it hot or cold? _____

2. To measure the thickness of a quarter, which unit of measurement would be used?

   ❑ mm   ❑ cm   ❑ km   ❑ m

3. How many ounces are in 2 gallons? _____

4. On the grid below, shade in an area of 16 square units.

5. How many ounces are in 2 pounds?

   ❑ 16   ❑ 8   ❑ 32

---

0 to 1 ✖, put a check in the chart on page 65 and go to the next page. 2 or more ✖ s, stop here and review skills; retest at a later date.

Geometry

Fifth Grade

1. If a circle has a radius of 4 1/2 inches, what would the diameter be?

   _____

2. What is the perimeter of an octagon where each size measures four inches?

   _____

3. How many faces does a pyramid have?

   _____

4. Which of the following is an obtuse angle? Circle your answer.

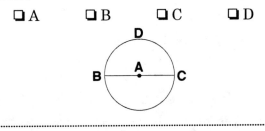

5. Which letter represents the circumference of the circle?

   ❏ A   ❏ B   ❏ C   ❏ D

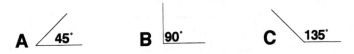

---

0 to 1 ✗, put a check in the chart on page 65 and go to the next page. 2 or more ✗ s, stop here and review skills; retest at a later date.

Fractions & Decimals

Write the decimal or fraction for each problem.

1. $\dfrac{1}{20}$ _____

2. .20 _____

3. $\dfrac{3}{4}$ _____

Solve the following decimal problems.

4. .75 + .5 = _____

5. .5 − .25 = _____

Write the following as percentages.

6. 6/8 _____

7. .66 _____

8. 15/25 _____

9. 4/10 _____

10. .17 _____

0 to 2 ✗ s, put a check in the chart on page 65 and go to the next page. 3 or more ✗ s, stop here and review skills; retest at a later date.

Word Problems

Fifth Grade

Read the following questions and write the correct answer.

1. Nick spent 1 hour and 15 minutes washing 75 dishes. what was the average time spent on each dish?_____

2. Each gray pebble in a box of 20 pebbles weighs 22 grams. Each black pebble in another box of 20 pebbles weighs 0.5 as much. How much do the black pebbles weigh altogether?_____

3. Sarah sold 3 large shiitake mushrooms for $10 a pound. They weigh 21 oz., 23 oz., 20 oz. How much did she make?_____

4. Kathleen had 27 concerts during January and February. She had twice as many concerts in February as in January. How many concerts did she have in February?_____

5. The baseball game started at 1:17 p.m. The two teams played for 2 hours and 54 minutes. At what time did the game end?_____

0 to 1 ✖, put a check in the chart on page 65 and go to the next page. 2 or more ✖s, stop here and review skills; retest at a later date.

Answer Key

Fourth grade assessment

page

53	**1.** 10	**2.** 30	**3.** 100	**4.** 500	**5.** 3
	6. 2	**7.** 3	**8.** 3 feet	**9.** 5 days	**10.** $8

54	**1.** 416	**2.** 2623	**3.** 1053	**4.** 3640	**5.** 2275
	6. 5 R50	**7.** .13	**8.** 7	**9.** 5 R1	**10.** 5

55	**1.** 1/2	**2.** 1/3	**3.** 3/4	**4.** >	**5.** >
	6. =	**7.** 1	**8.** 4	**9.** 4 1/2	**10.** 1 5/6
	11. 1 1/2	**12.** 7	**13.** 1 1/2	**14.** 4 5/6	

56	**1.** a gallon	**2.** 1,000	**3.** mm	**4.** km	**5.** <

57	**1.** 1 in 3	**2.** 150 ft	**3.** 5 vans	**4.** 1/2	**5.** three

Fifth grade assessment

page

58	**1.** 1	**2.** 6/25	**3.** 9/81 or 1/9		**4.** 8/24
or 1/3	**5.** 3/4	**6.** 4/3 or 1 1/3		**7.** 10/6 or 1 2/3	
	8. 20/24 or 5/6		**9.** 70/10 or 7		**10.** 6/5
or 1 1/5					

59	**1.** 24	**2.** 5	**3.** 23	**4.** 1/4	**5.** 1/8
60	**1.** 27	**2.** $3.50	**3.** 7	**4.** 147	**5.** 30.4
61	**1.** 2.8 cm	**2.** 3.2 cm	**3.** ---	**4.** 8	**5.** 20
62	**1.** 240cm	**2.** 16 in.	**3.** 6	**4.** 90°	**5.** AC

63	**1.** .6	**2.** 2/5	**3.** .25	**4.** .75	**5.** .5
	6. 70%	**7.** 80 %	**8.** 25%	**9.** 55%	**10.** 78%
64	**1.** 3	**2.** 3	**3.** $12	**4.** 12:05	**5.** 1/4

Fourth grade reassessment

page

| 159 | **1.** 10 | **2.** 30 | **3.** 200 | **4.** 400 | **5.** 4 |
| | **6.** 3 | **7.** 2 | **8.** 5 feet | **9.** 5 days | **10.** $4 |

| 160 | **1.** 1325 | **2.** 1392 | **3.** 2793 | **4.** 7553 | **5.** 121 |
| | **6.** 44 R2 | **7.** .15 R30 | **8.** 7 | **9.** 3 R58 | **10.** 12R20 |

161	**1.** 3/4	**2.** 2/3	**3.** 4/5	**4.** >	**5.** >
	6. =	**7.** 1 2/3	**8.** 4	**9.** 2 2/3	**10.** 1 1/2
	11. 4/5	**12.** 12	**13.** 8/9	**14.** 4 4/5	

| 162 | **1.** a quart | **2.** feet | **3.** ounces | **4.** cm | **5.** < |

| 163 | **1.** 1 in 5 | **2.** 1/6 | **3.** 4 buses | **4.** 5/8 | **5.** 1/8 |

Fifth grade reassessment

page

164	**1.** 2/9	**2.** 3/20	**3.** 10/12 or 5/6		**4.** 1/64
	5. 3/2 or 1 1/2		**6.** 2/6 or 1/3		**7.** 7/80
	8. 3/8	**9.** 1	**10.** 1/25		

165	**1.** 25	**2.** 4	**3.** Ella	**4.** 1/4	**5.** 1/4
166	**1.** 28	**2.** $3.50	**3.** 4	**4.** 43	**5.** 30.6
167	**1.** hot	**2.** mm	**3.** 256	**4.** ----	**5.** 32
168	**1.** 9 in.	**2.** 16 in.	**3.** 4	**4.** 135°	**5.** D
169	**1.** .5	**2.** 1/5	**3.** .75	**4.** 1.25	**5.** .25
	6. 75%	**7.** 66%	**8.** 60%	**9.** 40%	**10.** 17%
170	**1.** 1 min.	**2.** 220 gr.	**3.** $40	**4.** 18	**5.** 4:11

Appendix 1

NAEP Math Achievement Standards

The National Assessment of Educational Progress (NAEP) is an arm of the U.S. Department of Education that monitors academic achievement through periodic testing of 4th, 8th, and 12th graders. It serves the vital function of reporting to educators, parents, policy makers, and the general public how well our students are achieving in the area of math proficiency.

The 1992 NAEP Math Assessment was administered to national samples of 4th-, 8th-, and 12th-grade students attending public and nonpublic schools, and to samples of 4th graders in the jurisdictions that participated in the 1992 Trial State Assessment. Nearly 250,000 students were assessed in the national and jurisdiction samples. Students' math performance is described on a proficiency scale ranging from 0 to 500, and in relation to three achievement levels: *Basic, Proficient,* and *Advanced.* The assessment results are reported based on the performance of students at each of the three grades and within specific subgroups of the population. For each grade, the definitions are cumulative from *Basic* through *Advanced*. One level builds on the previous level. That is, knowledge at the *Proficient* level presumes mastery of the *Basic* level, and knowledge at the *Advanced* level presumes mastery of both the *Basic* and *Proficient* levels. The 5 NAEP content areas are:

1. Numbers and Operations
2. Measurement
3. Geometry
4. Data Analysis, Statistics, and Probability
5. Algebra and Functions

At the 4th grade level, algebra, and functions are treated in informal and exploratory ways, often through the study of patterns.

NAEP Scoring System: Fourth Grade Math Achievement Levels

Fourth-grade students performing at the *Basic* level should be able to estimate and use basic facts to perform simple computations with whole numbers, show some understanding of fractions and decimals, and solve some simple real-world problems in all NAEP content areas. Students at this level should be able to use—though not always accurately—four-function calculators, rulers, and geometric shapes. Their written responses are often minimal and presented without supporting information. Fourth graders performing at the *Proficient* level should be able to use whole numbers to estimate, compute, and determine whether results are reasonable. They should have a conceptual understanding of fractions and decimals be able to solve real-world problems in all NAEP content areas and use four-function calculators, rulers, and geometric shapes appropriately. They should employ problem-solving strategies such as identifying and using appropriate information. Their written solutions should be organized and presented both with supporting information and explanations of how they were achieved.

Fourth-grade students performing at the *Advanced* level should be able to solve complex and nonroutine real-world problems in all NAEP content areas. They should display mastery in the use of four-function calculators, rulers, and geometric shapes. These students are expected to draw logical conclusions and justify answers and solution processes by explaining why, as well as how, they were achieved. They should go beyond the obvious in their interpretations and be able to communicate their thoughts clearly and concisely.

Math achievement levels: United States
Grade 4: NAEP Trial State Assessments in Math

1996 Assessment, Public Schools Only

State	At or Above Basic	Below Basic
Alabama	48%	52%
Alaska	65%	35%
Arizona	57%	43%
Arkansas	54%!	46%!
California	46%	54%
Colorado	67%	33%
Connecticut	75%	25%
Delaware	54%	46%
District of Columbia	20%	80%
Florida	55%	45%
Georgia	53%	47%
Hawaii	53%	47%
Idaho	64%*	36%*

How Well Does Your Child Do Math?

Indiana	72%	28%
Iowa	74%	26%
Kentucky	60%	40%
Louisiana	44%	56%
Maine	75%	25%
Maryland	59%	41%
Massachusetts	71%	29%
Michigan	68%	32%
Minnesota	76%	24%
Mississippi	42%	58%
Missouri	66%	34%
Montana	71%	29%
Nebraska	70%	30%
Nevada	57%	43%
New Hampshire	74%*	26%*
New Jersey	68%	32%
New Mexico	51%	49%
New York	64%	36%
North Carolina	64%	36%
North Dakota	75%	25%
Ohio	59%*	41%*
Oklahoma	62%*	38%*
Oregon	65%	35%
Pennsylvania	68%	32%
Rhode Island	61%	39%
South Carolina	48%	52%
Tennessee	58%	42%
Texas	69%	31%
Utah	69%	31%
Vermont	67%	33%
Virginia	62%	38%
Washington	67%	33%
West Virginia	63%	37%
Wisconsin	74%	26%
Wyoming	64%	36%
Guam	28%	72%

! Statistical tests involving this value should be interpreted with caution. Standard error estimates may not be accurately determined and/or the sampling distribution of the statistics does not match statistical test assumptions. (See NAEP Report Appendix A)

* 1992 data

Source: NAEP 1996 Math Report Card for the Nation and the States. U.S. Department of Education, Office of Educational Research and Improvement

Math achievement levels: International
TIMSS Third International Math & Science Study

1996 Assessment, 41 Countries, Grades 7 and 8

Country	8th Grade Average Achievement	Country	7th Grade Average Achievement
Singapore	643	Singapore	601
Korea	607	Korea	577
Japan	605	Japan	571
Hong Kong	588	Hong Kong	564
Belgium (Fl)	565	Belgium (Fl)	558
Czech Republic	564	Czech Republic	523
Slovak Republic	547	Netherlands	516
Switzerland	545	Bulgaria	514
Netherlands	541	Austria	509
Slovenia	541	Slovak Republic	508
Bulgaria	540	Belgium (Fr)	507
Austria	539	Switzerland	506
France	538	Hungary	502
Hungary	537	Russian Federation	501
Russian Federation	535	Ireland	500
Australia	530	Slovenia	498
Ireland	527	Australia	498
Canada	527	Thailand	495
Belgium (Fr)	526	Canada	494
Thailand	522	France	492
Israel	522	Germany	484
Sweden	519	Sweden	477
Germany	509	England	476
New Zealand	508	United States	476
England	506	New Zealand	472
Norway	503	Denmark	465
Denmark	502	Scotland	463
United States	500	Latvia(LSS)	462
Scotland	498	Norway	461
Latvia (LSS)	493	Iceland	459
Spain	487	Romania	454
Iceland	487	Spain	448
Greece	484	Cyprus	446
Romania	482	Greece	440
Lithuania	477	Lithuania	428
Cyprus	474	Portugal	423
Portugal	454	Iran, Islamic Rep.	401
Iran, Islamic Rep.	428	Colombia	369
Kuwait	92	South Africa	348

Appendix 2

Online Educational Resources

National Education Association
http://www.nea.org

Interested in great schools? You've come to the right place. We're the more than 2.3 million members of the National Education Association, and we hope this page can help public education work for every child and every family.

EdWeb—Exploring Technology and School Reform
http://k12.cnidr.org:90/

Hunt down online educational resources around the world, learn about trends in education policy and information, examine success stories of computers in the classroom, and much more. Sponsored by The Corporation for Public Broadcasting and The Center for Networked Information Discovery and Retrieval.

The EdWeb K-12 Resource Guide
http://k12.cnidr.org:90/k12.html

This section of EdWeb offers a collection of the best online educational resources available, including teacher discussion groups and administrative services

Daily Report Card

http://www.utopia.com/mailings/reportcard/index.html

A summary of news in K-12 education from the National Education Goals Panel.

Educational Online Services (EOL)

http://netspace.students.brown.edu/eos/main_image.html

Welcome to the world wide web of educational online sources. This is a space where everyone can contribute and build a clearinghouse for educational information.

Research and Reference Resources

United States Department of Education

http://www.ed.gov
http://www.ed.gov./index.html

The site of the U.S. Department of Education. It lists news, grant and contract information, programs and services, publications and products, and other sites among more.

The U.S. Education Department/OERI

gopher://gopher.ed.gov

An information server that acts as a reference desk for all things educational. Includes educational software, Goals 2000 information, and primary, secondary, and vocational information.

Voluntary National Tests—Department of Education

http://www.ed.gov/nationaltests

The President proposed in his State of the Union Address on February 4, 1997 a voluntary, annual reading test in English at grade 4 and a math test at grade 8. These tests will provide parents and teachers with information about how their students are progressing compared to other states, the nation, and other countries.

The AskERIC Virtual Library

gopher://ericir.syr.edu

ERIC/AskERIC's information server contains select resources for both education and general use. Includes lesson plans, ERIC digests, infoguides and publications, reference tools, government information, and educational archives.

ERIC Clearinghouse on Assessment and Evaluation
http://ericae2.educ.cua.edu

This is a very extensive collection of information including assessment, evaluation, statistics, and educational research. Sponsored by the Catholic University of America.

UCLA's National Center for Evaluation, Standards, and Student Testing (CRESST)
Gopher://spinoza.cse.ucla.edu
Gopher://spinoza.cse.ucla.edu:71/11/AltAssessment

This is one of the best Web sites for K-12 educational research. You can find newsletters and technical reports. While the reports generally deal with research about alternative testing techniques (and are definitely worth reading because of that), several refer to the alignment between testing and standards.

Library of Congress
http://lc.loc.gov

Every book that has ever been published is referenced here.

Internet Resources Relating to Education
http://www.ilt.columbia.edu/net/guides/ILTeduc.html

Columbia University's education resource list. ILT is the Institute for Learning Technologies.

State-by-State Information

American Federation of Teachers (AFT)
http://www.aft.org
http://www.aft.org//research/reports/standards/iv.htm

The American Federation of Teachers (AFT) issued *Making Standards Matter 1996 An Annual 50-State Report on Efforts to Raise Academic Standards*. Nearly every state is working to set common academic standards for their students, but the AFT report makes it clear that most states have more work to do to strengthen their standards. For a report on an individual state, go online for the AFT state-by-state analysis.

State Curriculum Frameworks and Content Standards
http://www.ed.gov/offices/OERI/statecur

Brief description of various proposed frameworks and standards projects prepared with funding from DOE and Eisenhower National Program for Mathematics and Science Education

Developing Educational Standards: Overview
http://putwest.boces.org/Standards.html#TOC

An annotated list of Internet sites with K-12 educational standards and curriculum frameworks documents, run by the Putnam Valley Schools, Putnam Valley, NY. The three main sections are: governmental and general resources, listing by subject, listing by state.

Developing Educational Standards: Math
http://putwest.boces.org/StSu/Math.html

Developing Educational Standards is an annotated list of Internet sites with K-12 educational standards and curriculum frameworks documents.

National Network of Regional Educational Laboratories

Appalachian Region (AEL) Specialty: Rural Education
http://www.ael.org

Western Region (WestEd) Specialty: Assessment and Accountability
http://www.fwl.org

Central Region (McREL) Specialty: Curriculum, Learning and Instruction
http://www.mcrel.org

Midwestern Region (NCREL) Specialty: Technology
http://www.ncrel.org

Northwestern Region; Specialty: School Change Processes
http://www.nwrel.org

Pacific Region; Specialty: Language and Cultural Diversity
http://prel-oahu-1.prel.hawaii.edu/

Northeastern Region; Specialty: Language and Cultural Diversity
http://www.lab.brown.edu

Mid-Atlantic Region; Specialty: Urban Education
http://www.temple.edu/departments/LSS/

Southeastern Region; Specialty: Early Childhood Education
http://www.serve.org

Southwestern Region; Specialty: Language and Cultural Diversity
http://www.sedl.org

Mathematics

Mathematics for Parents
http://www.wcer.wisc.edu/Projects/Mathematics_and_Science/Modeling_in
_Math_and_Science/Newsletters/Table_of_Content.html

An extention of the Cognitively Guided Instruction (CGI) program. The goal of CGI is to inform teachers about how children think about simple arithmetic in the primary grades.

CONNECT—Every One Can Do Math and Science
http://bcn.boulder.co.us/connect/educators.html

Comprehensive resource and link list.

Eisenhower National Clearinghouse for Mathematics and Science Education (ENC)
http://www.enc.org

The Eisenhower National Clearinghouse has put together one of the richest and most valuable instructional resources for math and science education on the Internet. Short of having an extensive personal library, you cannot beat the breadth and quality of information ENC has made available here.

Math Mania—Exploring the Frontiers of Mathematics
http://csr.uvic.ca/~mmania

This site has sections on knots, graphs, sorting networks, and finite state machines.

National Council of Teachers of Mathematics (NCTM)
http://www.nctm.org

Founded in 1920 as a not-for-profit professional and educational association, NCTM is the largest organization dedicated to the improvement of mathematics education and to meeting the needs of teachers of mathematics. This site offers curriculum and evaluation standards for school mathematics.

Third International Math and Science Study (TIMSS)
http://ustimss.msu.edu

This site is funded by the National Science Foundation in conjunction with the National Center for Education Statistics. It contains a great deal of information about the Math and Science Study, as well as a wide range of links to other related sites.

NASA Education Sites
http://quest.arc.nasa.gov
http://quest.arc.nasa.gov/OER/EDRC22.htmlx
http://k12mac.larc.nasa.gov
http://www.nas.nasa.gov/HPCC/K12/edures.html

NASA and the High-Performance Computing and Communications Program offers a collection of servers specifically geared for teachers, students, and administrators. They offer math and science education resources, connectivity to numerous education servers, journals, and grant and project participation information.

National Science Foundation
gopher://stis.nsf.gov and http://stis.nsf.gov

NSF provides this gopher site as a source for educators and administrators. Contains information on NSF education projects, grants and publications.

American Mathematics Competitions (AMC)
http://www.unl.edu/amc

The American Mathematics Competitions (AMC) seek to increase interest in mathematics through friendly mathematics competitions for junior/middle and senior high school students.

Math Archives K-12 Index
http://archives.math.utk.edu/k12.html

A comprehensive listing of Internet sites containing significant collections of materials which can be used in the teaching of mathematics at the K-12 level.

Curriculum Consumers Education Service
http://www.rdc.udel.edu/CCIS/ccis_math.html

This site from the University of Delaware contains standards-based instructional resource profiles of various elements of a mathematical curriculum.

Appendix 3

Services and Resources

The services that follow are administered by the U.S. Department of Education to advance research, information, and communication about educational issues. Organizations should be contacted directly for more information about their research agenda and available services.

1. National Research and Development Centers

To help improve and strengthen student learning in the United States, the Office of Research supports 21 university-based national educational research and development Centers. The Centers are addressing specific topics such as early childhood education, student achievement in core academic subjects, teacher preparation and training, systemic education reform and restructuring, school governance and finance, postsecondary education and lifelong learning. In addition, most of the Centers are also focusing on the education of disadvantaged children and youth. Many Centers are collaborating with other universities, and many work with elementary and secondary schools. All are encouraged to make sure the information they produce makes a difference and reaches parents, teachers, and others who can use it to make meaningful changes in America's schools. Some of the centers include:

National Center for Research on
Educational Accountability and
Teacher Evaluation
Western Michigan University
401 B. Ellsworth Hall
Kalamazoo, MI 49008
616-387-5895

National Center for Research on
Cultural Diversity and Second
Language Learning
University of California at Santa
Cruz, Kerr Hall
Santa Cruz, CA 95064
408-459-3500

Center for Research on Effective
Schooling for Disadvantaged
Students
Johns Hopkins University
3505 North Charles St.
Baltimore, MD 21218
410-516-0370

National Research Center on
Education in the Inner Cities
Temple University
933 Ritter Hall Annex
13th St. and Cecil B. Moore Ave.
Philadelphia, PA 19122
215-204-3001

Center for Research on Evaluation,
Standards, and Student Testing
(CRESST)
University of California LA
Center for the Study of Evaluation
145 Moore Hall
Los Angeles, CA 90024-1522
310-206-1532

National Research Center on the
Gifted and Talented
University of Connecticut
362 Fairfield Rd. U-7
Storrs, CT 06269-2007
203-486-4826

National Center for Research in
Mathematical Sciences Education
University of Wisconsin at
Madison
Center for Education Research
1025 West Johnson St.
Madison, WI 53706
608-263-3605

National Center on Postsecondary
Teaching, Learning, and
Assessment
Pennsylvania State University
Center for the Study of Higher
Education
403 S. Allen St., Ste. 104
University Park, PA 16801-5252
814-865-5917

National Center for Science
Teaching and Learning
Ohio State University
1929 Kenny Rd.
Columbus, OH 43210-1015
614-292-3339

National Research Center on
Student Learning
University of Pittsburgh
Learning Research and
Development Center
3939 O'Hara St.
Pittsburgh, PA 15260
412-624-7457

2. ERIC Clearinghouses

Educational Resources Information Center (ERIC) is a nation-wide information network which acquires, catalogues, summarizes, and provides access to education information from all sources. ERIC produces a variety of publications and provides extensive user assistance, including AskERIC, an electronic question answering service for teachers on the Internet (askeric@ericir.syr.edu). The ERIC system includes 16 subject-specific Clearinghouses (some of which are listed below), the ERIC Processing and Reference facility.

Access ERIC maintains links to ERIC Clearinghouses and Adjunct Clearinghouses with WWW and/or Gopher sites. For more information call ACCESS ERIC 800-538-3742.

ERIC Clearinghouse on Assessment
and Evaluation
Catholic University of America
Department of Education
210 O'Boyle Hall
Washington, DC 20064-4035
202-319-5120

ERIC Clearinghouse on Educational
Management
University of Oregon
1787 Agate St.
Eugene, OR 97403-5207
503-346-5043

ERIC Clearinghouse on Rural
Education and Small Schools
1031 Quarrier St., Box 1348
Charleston, WV 25325-1348
304-347-0465

ERIC Clearinghouse on Higher
Education
George Washington University
One Dupont Circle NW, Ste. 630
Washington, DC 20036-1183
202-296-2597

ERIC Clearinghouse on Science,
Math & Environmental Education
Ohio State University
1929 Kenny Rd.
Columbus, OH 43210-1080
614-292-6717

ERIC Clearinghouse on Urban
Education
Columbia University
Main Hall, Rm. 300
525 W. 120th St.
New York, NY 10027-9998
212-678-3433

ERIC Clearinghouse on Elementary
and Early Childhood Education
University of Illinois
805 W. Pennsylvania Ave.
Urbana, IL 61801-4897
217-333-1386

ERIC Clearinghouse on Counseling
and Student Services
UNC Greensboro
School of Education, Curry Bldg.
Greensboro, NC 27412-5001
919-334-4114

ERIC Clearinghouse on Disabilities
and Gifted Education
Council for Exceptional Children
1920 Association Dr.
Reston, VA 22091-1589
703-264-9474

ERIC Clearinghouse on Information
and Technology, Syracuse Univ.
Ctr. for Science and Technology
4th Floor, Room 194
Syracuse, NY 13244-4100
315-443-3640

3. National Center for Education Statistics Data Sets

The National Center for Education Statistics collects data on many educational areas. What follows are brief descriptions of some NCES data sets. For a complete description of all of their data sets, contact OERI at 800-424-1616 for a copy of NCES Programs.

National Assessment of Educational Progress (NAEP) provides data on the educational attainment of U.S. students. It serves as a "report card" on the national condition of education. Students are assessed at grades 4, 8, and 12 in reading and writing and subject areas that include math, science, U.S. history, and world geography. Contact: Education Assessment Division, 202-219-1761

Common Core of Data (CCD) is a comprehensive, annual, national statistical database of all public elementary and secondary schools and school districts, which contains data that are comparable across all states. Contact: Elementary and Secondary Education Statistics Division, 202-219-1335

4. National Information Center for Children and Youth with Disabilities (NICHCY)

NICHCY provides information and technical assistance free of charge to families, professionals, caregivers, advocates, agencies, and others in helping children and youth with disabilities to become participating members of the community. NICHCY offers databases, publications and newsletters, updated fact sheets, briefing papers, and parents' guides. Contact: NICHCY/Suzanne Ripley, P.O. Box 1492, Washington, DC 20013, 800-695-0285

5. Eisenhower National Clearinghouse for Mathematics and Science Education (ENC)

The Eisenhower National Clearinghouse for Mathematics and Science Education is the National Repository for K-12 mathematics and science instructional materials and an online searchable resource of descriptions of those materials and virtual resources, hot links to outstanding virtual resources for math and science teaching, and Federal programs supporting math and science education improvement. Contact: ENC/Len Simutis, Eisenhower National Clearinghouse, The Ohio State University, 1929 Kenny Rd., Columbus, OH 43210-1079, 614-292-7784.

Index